Dyslexia and Self-concept
Seeking a dyslexic identity

Dyslexia and Self-concept

Seeking a dyslexic identity

ROBERT BURDEN PhD
University of Exeter

Consultant Editor
MARGARET SNOWLING
University of York

W
WHURR PUBLISHERS
LONDON AND PHILADELPHIA

© 2005 Whurr Publishers Ltd
First published 2005
by Whurr Publishers Ltd
19b Compton Terrace
London N1 2UN England and
325 Chestnut Street, Philadelphia PA 19106 USA

British Library Cataloguing in Publication Data

A catalogue record for this book
is available from the British Library.

ISBN 1 86156 483 X

Contents

Preface

This book has been written with a particular purpose in mind: to find ways of enabling the thousands of people who have learning difficulties of a dyslexic nature to explain how it affects their lives. Books and research reports on dyslexia have multiplied in recent years, but few have sought to present the situation from the dyslexics' perspective. I hope that this book will provide a helpful step in redressing the balance, while at the same time offering a means for further research in this highly important area.

I have tried to write the book in a style that makes it accessible to a variety of audiences. As an academic, I want my findings to be taken as a significant contribution to public and professional knowledge about dyslexia and issues associated with the application of the term. As a trainer of teachers, I would like teachers at all stages of their careers to gain a greater depth of understanding of their role in empowering young people with dyslexic difficulties to become confident and autonomous learners. As an educational psychologist, I hope that dyslexic young people and their parents will feel that the book provides an accurate reflection of their thoughts and feelings.

For me, one of the most interesting aspects of writing the book has been the realisation that this has been just the first step in an ongoing series of research studies into the lives of dyslexic people. There is still a great deal to be said.

Bob Burden
December 2004

Acknowledgements

My thanks are due to:

Julia Burdett, who contributed so creatively to the research process, and without whom this book would not have been written;

Julie and Steve for their supportive encouragement and warm hospitality in welcoming us into their school;

the students who talked so openly and honestly about their experiences and in doing so opened our eyes to a totally new perspective on dyslexia;

Lucy Smith, who was completely unflappable in helping to bring this manuscript to completion on time in the face of my constant alterations and additions.

The search for a dyslexic identity

The title of this introduction reflects an unjustifiably neglected area of research and writing about the developmental tasks faced by children and young people whose learning careers are bedevilled by specific difficulties of a dyslexic nature. This somewhat convoluted sentence needs unpacking further because each phrase has been constructed to represent an aspect of the complex phenomenon commonly referred to in the United Kingdom and many parts of the world as dyslexia (but, in the USA, by the more generic term 'learning disability').

Firstly, the term 'unjustifiably neglected' refers to the fact that by far the bulk of research reports and papers published over the past ten years with dyslexia as their main topic have dwelt upon two issues, causation and remediation. This is not to deny the importance of research into the key role played by the establishment of phonological awareness, or of the influence of the cerebellum on developing literacy skills, nor to dismiss the influence of the growing multitude of books on multi-sensory training and other remedial measures. What is contested, however, is the neglect of the human side of dyslexia in much of this writing and the lack of consideration given to the needs of the whole child in coming to understand their difficulties and learning how to deal with them appropriately. In this respect, the situation has changed little over the past decade since Maughan (1994) pointed to the relative absence of research into the relationship between reading and emotion.

It is a well-established fact that all children are expected to reach similar developmental goals as they pass through different phases of their lives from childhood to maturity. For children with disabilities, however, these goals may well prove more difficult to achieve due to some specific aspect of their disability. There are many eminent

1

psychologists such as Eric Erikson and Carl Rogers who argue that the establishment of a secure and positive sense of identity, sometimes referred to as 'ego integrity', can only be achieved through the successful accomplishment of these key developmental tasks. Other psychologists, from William James onwards, describe this as the development of the self-concept, which is itself made up of a number of different 'selves', such as the intellectual, the physical, the emotional, the social, the academic and the moral self. The important point here is that difficulties in coming to terms with any one of these areas may well have profound effects on some or all of the others. The fundamental issues to be addressed by this book are concerned with the importance of the self-concept and self-esteem in the development of a positive or negative sense of dyslexic identity and with the factors that are most significant in influencing this.

The child with dyslexia is often faced with a further set of problems described by the sociologist Erving Goffman as 'marginalizing' (Goffman, 1968). This suggests that coping in school or social situations can sometimes be more difficult for children with unrecognized or misunderstood disabilities than it is for those with more readily explicable difficulties. In many, even most, ways they can and do 'pass' as normal and therefore their unexpected difficulties prove to be even more puzzling to themselves and significant others such as their parents and teachers.

There is an increasing body of evidence to show that children with difficulties of a dyslexic nature are at particular risk of developing distorted or damaged self-concepts as a result of their marginalized status, particularly if the specific nature of their difficulties is not recognized at an early stage in their school careers. Furthermore, unless steps are taken to enable the dyslexic child to understand and deal with their difficulties in a holistic manner, i.e. one that involves all aspects of the child's development, it will become increasingly difficult to overcome the detrimental effects of a negative self-image, not just at school but in later life as well. It is here that we can see the importance of the notion of a 'learning career', a concept that is aptly illustrated by Stanovich's reference to the 'Matthew effect' whereby 'to those who hath shall be given; from those who hath not shall be taken away', i.e. that early difficulties at school in establishing the basic skills of literacy and/or numeracy are likely to have a cumulative effect in making it extremely difficult for such children ever to catch up (Stanovich, 1986).

It is important at this early juncture to emphasize that when we use such terms as 'dyslexics' or 'dyslexic children' we are using a form of convenient shorthand to refer to children or adults with specific learning difficulties of a dyslexic nature. In employing these terms I am nevertheless aware that apart from manifesting such difficulties in certain situations, a person with dyslexia is not necessarily different from anyone else in the general population. At the same time, I am also aware that there is a danger of stigmatizing the whole person by using such descriptive terms or phrases and, in doing so, affecting their overall self-concept.

Readers are therefore urged to bear this caveat in mind as they work their way through the book; otherwise there is danger of providing an ongoing contradiction to one of the main messages that I am seeking to impart.

One further issue to be explored is the potential contribution of recent theoretical perspectives from the social sciences to our understanding of the dyslexic phenomenon and, in particular, of how those with dyslexic difficulties make sense of and can be helped to overcome the problems they encounter as a result of their dyslexia. Again, it is a surprising fact that much of the research on dyslexia has been extremely narrow in its theoretical orientation, reflecting a limited focus on the brain and language/literacy development which is somewhat out of step with current psychological and sociological perspectives on human development.

As Herrington and Hunter-Carsh have noted (2001, p. 114), 'The dominant paradigm is still one of "in-person" weakness rather than one which shows quite clearly that it is the specific values which are attached to particular concepts and standards of literacy and numeracy which largely shape the way in which dyslexia is perceived and experienced. It is substantially these perspectives which make dyslexia disabling.'

The book begins, therefore, with an overview of some main theories describing the nature and importance of the self-concept together with ways in which a positive sense of self-identity is developed throughout the lifespan. This is followed by a summary of what little research currently exists on the self-concept of dyslexic children and adults, emphasizing in particular the dangers associated with accumulated feelings of learned helplessness and depression and introducing the notion of a developing sense of *dyslexic identity*. Chapter 2 provides an introduction to some recent theoretical perspectives on learning and describes more fully key psychological concepts related to aspects of self-perception and self-esteem. The case is made that such an approach can provide a helpful starting point in attempting to construct a picture of individuals' and groups' developing sense of identity. It also enables us to identify and construct useful techniques for assessing young people's perceptions of themselves as learners and problem-solvers, and enabling them to describe the development of their feelings of self-efficacy, learned helplessness and depression. The construction and use of such techniques are described in Chapter 3.

Chapter 4 reveals how the results of interviews with 50 dyslexic boys were analysed to produce a model framework for describing their learning careers and the development of their sense of identity. This in turn is followed, in Chapter 5, by descriptions of their academic self-concepts and feelings of self-efficacy, learned helplessness and depression both at a general level and by means of individual narratives. Some tentative conclusions are made which draw upon current psychological theories to relate the positive sense of dyslexic 'pride' demonstrated by these students in the ethos of the school and its academic success rate. Chapter 6 uses case histories to illustrate both the similarities in the emerging themes and the uniqueness of each boy's personal story.

The final chapter draws together the various strands of the research to summarize the key findings and propose a blueprint for the construction of a positive dyslexic identity. In particular, it also focuses on the potential contribution of *mediated learning experiences* in this endeavour.

CHAPTER 1

The self-concept and its relationship to educational achievement

One of the most important questions with which each of us is faced at various times in our lives is, 'Who am I?' As young children develop they gradually become more and more aware that whilst there are many ways in which they are similar to other boys and girls, there are at least as many ways in which they differ. This realization, which is largely shaped by the social and cultural context into which they are born and the nature of their interactions with significant others in their lives, leads to the construction of each person's unique sense of identity. It has been suggested by the psychologist Eric Erikson that during the period of adolescence one of the most vital tasks for every individual is to establish a sense of 'ego integrity', a firm grasp of who we are and what we want to become. For Erikson the resolution of the adolescence identity crisis is essential to enable a person to continue to mature and lead a satisfying and fulfilling life. At the same time, he considers that whether or not such a resolution is reached will depend upon how well the individual has passed through a series of earlier developmental stages. Thus our early childhood experiences are considered to play a significant part in our attitudes towards ourselves and our place in the world (Erikson, 1959).

This shaping of a sense of identity is referred to by others as the construction of the self-concept, which has been defined by another psychologist, Carl Rogers, as: 'composed of such elements as the perceptions of one's characteristics and abilities: the percepts and concepts of the self in relation to others and to the environments; the value qualities which are perceived as associated with experiences and objects; and the goals and ideas which are perceived as having positive or negative valence' (Rogers, 1951, p. 138). A more succinct definition offered by Robert Burns (1982, p. 7) is that 'self-concept is best regarded as a dynamic complex of attitudes held towards themselves by each person'.

5

Jerome Bruner (1996) has suggested that sense of self is more or less equal to the individual's 'conception of their own powers'. This has been interpreted elsewhere as meaning that 'to know one's self is to appreciate one's capacities in different circumstances – to evaluate one's stream of thought and action as they fit into surrounding realities' (Reed, 2001, p. 121). One implication of such a definition is that education is less likely to lead to some kind of permanent change in the private self, as to an adaptation of the self within and to a variety of contexts. The two key properties of self-identification by Bruner are those of *agency* and *evaluation*, with agency referring to the guidance of action by external, often shared, meanings and values, and evaluation used to refer to how well one's agency meshes with others' actions.

In his seminal work, *Self-concept Development and Education*, Burns (1982) put forward the suggestion that self-concept can be identified as a compound of two elements, self-image and self-evaluation. By looking at it in this way, we can see that it has many of the attributes of an attitude that people develop about themselves. Attitudes are usually considered to consist of three key elements: the cognitive, the connative and the behavioural, or, in more basic terms, the beliefs that we hold about something or someone, the strengths of our feelings towards or against that object or person, and our predisposition to act in certain ways.

It can be seen, therefore, that our self-image is the set of beliefs that we hold about various aspects of ourselves, how we look, how we get on with others, how good we are at various aspects of schoolwork and so on. Our evaluation of these beliefs, how strongly they matter to us, is what we usually mean when we refer to self-esteem.

The third major aspect of an attitude is the predisposition that it gives us to act in certain ways. If I believe something to be true and it matters a great deal to me, then I will be inclined to act accordingly when faced with an issue of this nature. As far as our self-concept is concerned, the images that we construct about certain significant aspects of ourselves and the strength of feeling that we have about those aspects will be likely to affect our behaviour in circumstances where such thoughts and feelings are pertinent. If I believe that I am a skilful games player and games playing is an important activity for me, I am likely to enter into games with some confidence of a successful outcome and will do my best to succeed.

A problem that immediately arises here is that there are practically limitless numbers of ways in which we can perceive ourselves.

Psychologists have tended to focus upon six or eight major categories, but then disagree as to whether our self-image/self-esteem in each of these categories is cumulative, thereby producing an overall sense of global self-concept (GSC), or whether our thoughts and feelings about each of these individual aspects of ourselves exist relatively independently of each other. Does how I see myself as a parent or a friend necessarily have any connection with how I see myself as a musician or an academic? This is an important point because much of the research into the relationship between self-concept and other attributes such as achievement has been bedevilled by confusion as to exactly what is being measured. As Hansford and Hattie (1982) point out in their meta-analysis of research studies into the relationship between people's self-perceptions and their academic achievements, terms such as self-concept, self-image and self-esteem are often used interchangeably without adequate definition, and applied without valid and reliable measurement techniques. We therefore need to be clear as to exactly what aspect of self-concept we are particularly interested in and exactly how we intend to measure this. At the same time, we need to try to assess how specific aspects of our self-concept are shaped and whether there is a more general spreading effect to other areas of our developing sense of identity. In this book, for reasons which will become clear later, we shall be focusing on dyslexic young people's conceptions of themselves as learners and problem-solvers and the effect this can have upon their approach to learning and their eventual success or failure in their learning endeavours.

As Burns makes clear, the self-concept is a set of subjectively constructed attributes and feelings, which take on their meanings for an individual through the general evaluation of that quality or attribute in their particular society. It therefore follows that those of us who possess— characteristics considered to be socially undesirable will begin to perceive ourselves as undesirable or in some way wanting. Since literacy is— considered to be a highly desirable characteristic in our society, those who have difficulty in becoming literate will automatically find it difficult to develop positive academic self-concepts, particularly if we accept the premise that our self-evaluations are determined by our beliefs about how others see us. This is usually referred to as 'the looking glass self', a term that was first constructed in the early years of the twentieth century (Cooley, 1912).

Burns suggests further that the self-concept appears to have a threefold role: maintaining a sense of inner consistency, determining how experiences are interpreted, and providing a set of expectancies. The first role relates to what has sometimes been termed 'the principle of homeostasis'. It has been argued by many psychologists that, in order to survive, human beings need to establish a sense of inner harmony and equilibrium. This will be closely associated with what individuals think and feel about themselves and they will act in ways which are consistent with this. If we find again and again that we have difficulties in coping successfully with a culturally valued activity such as reading or spelling, we are likely to explain this to ourselves in terms of some enduring trait such as 'stupidity' and to begin to act in other situations in ways which confirm this. Burns argues that the maintenance of the self-concept, positive or negative, appears to be a prime motivator in all normal behaviour. In this he differs in some important ways from *symbolic interactionists*, who hold the view that our self-concept can and does shift as a result of our experiences in interacting with significant others (Pollard, 1996). As we shall see, belief in the consistency of one's self-concept is of particular significance to children struggling to overcome learning difficulties of a dyslexic nature. –

The second important role performed by the self-concept is the way in which it shapes our interpretation of experiences, i.e. it plays an important part in helping us to make sense of and give meaning to what happens to us. If I have a negative academic self-concept, I am more likely to interpret my failure on a learning task, such as a spelling test, in global terms rather than as a one-off experience. Burns makes the important point that there is no action that a teacher can take that a child with a negative self-concept cannot interpret in a negative way. For this reason, merely providing praise or other forms of positive reinforcement will not be sufficient to change that child's view of him-/herself. It takes much more deep-rooted action to bring about positive change in how we see ourselves.

Expectancy theory suggests that we all carry with us a set of expectations about the world which determine how we are most likely to act. If we expect to have positive experiences we will act in ways that will bring them about. If we expect negative experiences we will similarly act in ways to make these happen. Thus, if a dyslexic child's academic self-concept is one that leads the child to expect failure in learning to read and/or spell, then he or she is likely to act in ways that will make this a self-fulfilling prophecy.

It is not difficult to see, therefore, how important a positive academic self-concept is likely to be in affecting the behaviour and expectancies of dyslexic children with regard to becoming literate, and how difficult it can be to change negative self-perceptions once they have been formed. Burns (1982) reports a number of research studies which show that underachievers see themselves as less adequate and less acceptable to others. He also makes the point (p. 214) that 'Most experienced teachers can recite a great many examples in which a student's concept of his abilities severely restricts his achievement, even though his real abilities may be superior to those which he demonstrates'. So a particular self-perception can easily become self-validating such that a child who avoids reading thereby bypasses the very experience which might change their concept of self. Thus, these notions of inability to learn become self-fulfilling prophecies. Burns is compelled to conclude (p. 226) that 'Children whose self-concepts do not include the view that they can achieve academically tend to fulfil that prediction.'

It is here that we need to be clear about the distinction between self-concept and self-esteem. If children who are performing poorly at their schoolwork respond honestly to questions about their academic self-concept, their responses will inevitably be negative. This does not necessarily mean, however, that their academic self-esteem need be negative, although this is highly likely to be the case if doing well at school is important to them. Positive self-esteem is not merely a matter of feeling good about oneself. It consists of a much more deep-rooted belief in one's capability to overcome the problems with which one is faced, the confidence to deal with negative issues as they arise and a realistic sense of agency, i.e. that one has the skills and strategies to act in an effective manner when called upon to do so. Only by building up such attributes to overcome feelings of poor self-esteem and drawing upon them in one's approach to learning will a negative academic self-concept be changed into a realistically positive one. This is no easy task, but it is by no means impossible, as we shall see.

What do we know about the self-concepts of people with dyslexia?

Surprisingly, there appears to have been comparatively little research into how dyslexic children and adults make sense of their disability or how this affects their perceptions of themselves as learners or as (prospective) citizens of the world. This is even more surprising in view of what we know about the importance of self-perceptions in contributing to academic and more general success in life. We also know that continuing feelings of failure whilst at school can have life-long debilitating effects on individuals' ability to cope with stress (Lewandowski and Arcangelo, 1994).

In one adult study, Riddick and her co-workers found, by comparing the past and present educational histories of 16 dyslexic university students with matched controls, that the dyslexic group displayed significantly lower self-esteem than the controls (Riddick et al., 1999). The dyslexics also reported themselves as feeling more anxious and less competent in their written work whilst at school than their contemporaries and as carrying these feelings of incompetence with them into university. This finding endorsed that of previous researchers (e.g. Gerber et al., 1990).

Research has also shown us that adolescent poor readers tend to have low self-esteem and to feel themselves less valued members of their classes (Fairhurst and Pumfrey, 1992). This finding has been confirmed in a variety of different countries such as Norway, where a study of 3000 schoolchildren found that those with specific learning difficulties had lower self-esteem and self-confidence than their contemporaries (Gjessing and Karlsen, 1989), and the USA, where similar findings were obtained by Chapman (1988a). An important early study by Zimmerman and Allegrand (1965) compared the personality characteristics and attitudes towards achievement of two groups of poor ($n = 71$) and good ($n = 82$) readers equated as nearly as possible for age, sex, ethnic background and intelligence. Good readers were found to describe themselves as better adjusted, motivated and striving for success whilst the poor readers displayed feelings of discouragement, inadequacy and anxiety, and tended to set themselves ephemeral and short-term goals. More recently, Lerner (2000) has noted that as well as displaying underachievement during the elementary school years, children in the USA diagnosed as suffering from learning disabilities typically experience social-emotional problems such as low self-esteem and often struggle to make and maintain friendships. These problems are carried forward into adolescence where they can develop into learned helplessness, a significant drop in their confidence to learn and succeed, low motivation to achieve, attention problems and maladaptive behaviour.

Further confirmation of the potential negative consequences on the feelings of dyslexic children has been provided in a number of more personal accounts, mainly of a retrospective nature (e.g. Osmond, 1993; Edwards, 1994). Often, such accounts are of an impassioned nature, describing the slights, the injustices, the emotional pain and unbearable stress suffered by individual or small groups of dyslexics as a result of unfortunate childhood experiences and/or the ignorance of significant others. Whilst such accounts should never be ignored or devalued, their very lack of objectivity means that they cannot necessarily be taken as representative of the experiences of all or even the majority of dyslexic children. We need more carefully controlled investigations before we can begin to reach such conclusions, but the fact that these are representative accounts of the feelings of some dyslexic children should not be overlooked.

As was indicated earlier, controlled studies of the emotional effects of dyslexia on children or adults have been relatively rare compared with research into other aspects of dyslexia. In the USA, studies by Saracoglu et al. (1989) and Lewandowski and Arcangelo (1994) both reported low self-concepts/self-esteem in adults with learning disabilities and accompanying difficulties with emotional adjustment. Data from the British birth cohort longitudinal studies reported by Bynner and Ekynsmith (1994) showed a relationship between continuing literacy difficulties, or, more correctly, *perceived* literacy difficulties, and feelings of depression.

Frederickson and Jacobs (2001) compared the academic self-perceptions and attributions for success and failure of 20 children with dyslexia with 20 matched controls with no learning difficulties. They found that the dyslexic children displayed significantly lower academic self-concepts than their matched peers, but their global self-worth was not significantly lower. They also found that children with a strong internal locus of control tended to have higher academic self-concepts than those who saw their success and failure as outside their control, even when actual reading attainment was taken into account.

These findings confirm previous research findings, mainly carried out in the USA with children with learning disabilities (Resnick and Harter, 1989; Chapman, 1988b), especially when such children were educated in mainstream classrooms rather than in special classes. However, when Kistner et al. (1988) monitored the progress of children with specific learning difficulties over a period of two years, they found that those who attributed failure to factors within their control (e.g. effort) made the greater achievement gains. At the same time,

Jacobson et al. (1986) found that children with learning disabilities were more likely than normally achieving children to see both success and failure as due to factors outside their control.

The importance of focusing on domain-specific self-perceptions rather than on global self-esteem has been further emphasized by Carr et al. (1991). This point was supported by the findings of a study of the relationship between academic self-concept and achievement of 600 Norwegian primary school children (Skaalvik and Hagvet, 1990). The conclusion of these researchers was that academic self-concept acts as a mediating variable between academic performance and global self-esteem as well as providing a causal influence on academic achievement.

Attempts to measure dyslexic children's feelings about themselves have been fraught with difficulties, not least because of the lack of appropriate measurement techniques allied to meaningful psychological theories about dyslexic children's psychosocial development. Two studies (Thomson and Hartley, 1980; Humphrey, 2002) drew upon Kelly's Repertory Grid Technique in this endeavour with not altogether satisfactory results. A further study by Thomson reported in his book *Developmental Dyslexia* (1990), however, describes the use of a self-esteem inventory to compare the self-esteem of children who had spent a differential amount of time at a specialist school for dyslexics. He found that the social and academic self-esteem of the pupils increased considerably in accordance with the time spent at the school, whilst the initially high level of parental esteem remained constant.

Humphrey and Mullins (2002), in a more recent paper, emphasize the need to ground investigations in this area in sound psychological theory. They pinpoint, in particular, attribution theory, incorporating aspects of locus of control and learned helplessness. Briefly, attribution theory is concerned with the reasons to which individuals attribute their successes and failures in life, while locus of control relates to whether these reasons are perceived as *internal* and within the individual's own control, or *external* and in the control of more powerful other people or forces.

Learned helplessness is generally considered to be the state that people fall into when, usually as a result of constant failure, they feel that there is no point in making the effort to attempt tasks because of what they perceive as the inevitability of failure (Bar-Tal and Darom, 1979; Joiner and Wager, 1995). As Seligman (1991, p. 5) puts it,

'Helplessness is the state of affairs in which nothing you choose to do affects what happens to you'.

From the results of their own study, Humphrey and Mullins conclude that the experience of dyslexia has clear and demonstrable negative effects on the self-concept and self-esteem of children, adding that 'the parallels between learned helplessness and children with reading difficulties are striking' (2002, p. 197). In one of the very few published studies attempting to apply these ideas, Butkowsky and Willows (1980) claim to have found that good and poor readers display different attributional styles, with poor readers being more likely to blame themselves for failure and to attribute success to luck. Poor readers also appeared to have lower expectations of success and to respond more negatively to failure.

We can conclude with some confidence from this review of the somewhat limited research literature that:

- there is a clear negative association between early and continuing literacy difficulties and self-concept/self-esteem;
- these negative feelings are likely to be long-lasting;
- the ways in which they may manifest themselves are likely to be complex, taking the form of vulnerability to stress, feelings of learned helplessness and depression.

What we do not as yet know with any confidence is whether such effects are inevitable in the long or short term, or whether they can be alleviated and even overcome by particular kinds of intervention programmes. Reports on the outcomes of intervention programmes implemented with dyslexic children and adults have tended almost exclusively to focus upon measured gains in academic achievement without reporting the broader psychological effects on the participants in either the short or long term. As Riddick et al. (1999, p. 244) state in concluding their study, 'we need to identify those dyslexic students who are low in self-esteem and/or high in anxiety and evaluate what forms of environmental changes and support will be most effective in raising their self-esteem and lowering their anxiety . . . (therefore) . . . consideration could be given to using measures such as these as part of a student's overall assessment'. They add that measures of these psychological aspects could also be used to help monitor the effectiveness of various forms of intervention or support. Even more radically, Herrington and Hunter-Carsch make the point that 'there does not appear to be a broad-based attempt to integrate models of dyslexia with either radical perspectives of literacy or social models of disabilities' (Herrington and Hunter-Carsch, 2001, p. 114).

The next chapter will go on to consider some of these issues in greater detail. It will provide a more detailed description of key psychological concepts which can be drawn upon to help us make sense of how those suffering from learning disabilities such as dyslexia think and feel about themselves and the difficulties with which they are faced. These theoretical foundations will subsequently be used to identify and construct suitable instruments for exploring dyslexic children's developing sense of identity, their academic self-concepts and aspects of their academic self-esteem.

CHAPTER 2

A theoretical framework for investigating dyslexics' personal appraisal and sense of identity

As the father of personal construct psychology, George Kelly, is once supposed to have said, if you want to find out what somebody thinks or feels about something, why not ask them? They might just tell you. Despite such sound advice, it is surprising how infrequently it seems to have been taken on behalf of the dyslexic population. While there are literally thousands of articles and books written about the nature of dyslexia, its diagnosis and remediation, comparatively little has been written as a result of asking dyslexics about how they think and feel about their disabilities.

One reason for this state of affairs may well be that finding the right questions to ask has proved to be a lot more difficult than might first appear. What exactly is it that we want to know and how can we be sure that the answers we obtain are truly representative of dyslexics at large? Such questions relate to core issues of research methodology such as the construction of questionnaires and interview schedules, the validity and reliability of their items and the generalizability of their findings. Moreover, the strength of any investigative approach will undoubtedly be built upon the quality of the psychological theories upon which the questions are based and which will be used to make sense of the results.

In our research[1] we have drawn upon a number of major theories from the social sciences, specifically socio-cultural theory, symbolic interactionism, motivational and attitudinal theories, which in turn

---

[1] The research to be described in the following chapters, including the construction of the Dyslexia Identity Scale, was carried out in conjunction with my research assistant, Julia Burdett, thus accounting for the use of the plural personal pronoun.

15

_..._ given rise to such related constructs as self-efficacy, attribution, locus of control and learned helplessness. Each of these will now be described before turning to the techniques that have been developed for their assessment.

✗ Socio-cultural theory

Socio-cultural theory (sometimes referred to as social constructionism/constructivism) essentially takes the view that all knowledge is constructed (rather than transmitted) as a result of social interactions within specific cultural contexts. The point of importance for our understanding of dyslexia is that this suggests that dyslexics are not doomed to a lifetime of failure as a result of their genetic endowments or physiological inadequacies but may in a sense be victims of the social and educational mores that prevail in a particular place at a particular time, and that this is open to change. Moreover, this change is less likely to be brought about by instructional drills than by the construction of new shared meanings between a more knowledgeable person and the dyslexic novice.

This point has been expressed by James Wertsch in the following way:

> Social constructionist psychology suggests that the concepts, language and signs of the cultural context structure children's thinking and become internalised as 'voices of the mind'. They thus mediate action and new learning. (Wertsch, 1992, p. x)

The sociologist and educator Andrew Pollard has emphasized the close links between social constructionism and *symbolic interactionism*, which he describes as 'founded on the belief that people "act" on the basis of meanings and understandings which they develop through interaction with others. Human action is thus seen as having a social bias rather than deriving, for example, from instinct or genetics' (Pollard, 1996, p. xiii).

If we follow this line of reasoning we can see how the concept of 'self' emerges as children interpret the responses of other people to their actions, either verbally or non-verbally. In the words of Herrington and Hunter-Carsch (2001 p. 129), 'We know that the "disability" associated with dyslexia is largely constructed from the perceptions and social practices of others.' Coles takes this even further in his description of the potentially negative effect of ascribing a disability label to children:

> The children do not merely accept a label ascribed by others and then acquire the self-concept of being powerless to act accordingly. Rather in the activity of failing, of being unable to accomplish academic tasks, and in having their activity defined as being one exuding intellectual powerlessness, the child becomes powerless .... Being actually powerless means that the individual's actions will display learning disabled behaviour that will lead important overseers, such as teachers and parents, to respond to the child in ways that increase the learning disability. (Coles, 1987, p. 172)

Interactionists also argue that the sense of self is continually refined in later life and acts as a basis for thought and behaviour. A long-standing approach to understanding the development of a sense of self is Cooley's (1912) notion of the 'looking glass self', which can be seen to be closely akin to the ideas of the symbolic interactionists.

⚹ Motivation

Recent motivational theory provides us with a complementary approach (Williams et al., 2002), which relates directly to both social constructivism and symbolic interactionism. Here the emphasis is upon three factors; the individual's *attitude* towards what is to be learnt, their *self-concept as a learner* and their *sense of agency* or competence in being able to achieve what they set out to do. These *internal* factors are in turn influenced by such *external* factors as parental expectations, understanding and support, the mediational power of teachers and the reactions of the peer group and friends.

Table 2.1 provides a basic overview of how such a framework can encompass many of the theoretical approaches to motivation that currently exist in the psychological literature.

Key aspects of motivation

(a) Attitude

In the field of attitudes one theory stands out as relating directly to our current sphere of interest. This was first postulated by two social psychologists, Fishbein and Ajzen, in the 1970s as the *theory of reasoned action*, which proposed that the likelihood of any person acting in a

Table 2.1 Internal factors affecting motivation

Attitude	The self	Sense of agency
To learning in general	Self-image	Feelings of competence
To the subject area:	Self-concept	versus learned helplessness
perceived value	Self-esteem	Self-efficacy/perceived ability
personal relevance	Self-worth concern	Locus of control/causality
enjoyment	Anxiety	Attributions: perceived
interest	Effectiveness motivation	reasons for success or
To specific tasks/activities:	Motivational style	failure
challenge		Goal setting: mastery
optimal arousal		versus performance
		Available strategies:
		cognitive, metacognitive
		Effort and persistence

certain way is most likely to be determined by their *intention* to act in that way (Fishbein and Ajzen, 1975). This intention is itself influenced by the person's positive or negative attitude towards the action or behaviour in question and by prevailing societal norms, i.e. the perceived social pressure to perform or not perform the act. A further element of the theory was later added by Ajzen (1991) to form the *theory of planned behaviour* (TPB). This extra element, the notion of perceived behavioural control, refers to the degree to which individuals feel their action to be within their control rather than at the mercy of powerful events or other people. In this respect it is similar to the widely recognized and researched notion of *locus of control*. Research suggests that each of the three elements of TPB are strongly linked and together can account for some 20% of the variance in learning outcomes (Sutton, 1998; Armitage and Conner, 2001).

Figure 2.1 displays the key elements of the theory of planned behaviour in diagrammatical form.

How does this relate to the educational needs of dyslexic students? Basically, it suggests that if dyslexic students are to make substantial educational progress, they stand a much better chance of doing so if their attitude towards schooling in general, and literacy/numeracy in particular, is a positive one, if they are in an environment where personal goal-setting and striving for academic success is the shared norm amongst the pupils, and if they have a strong sense that their future success is in their own hands. If, on the other hand, they have

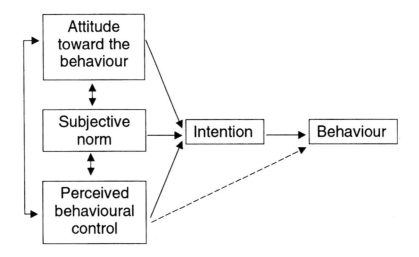

Figure 2.1 Ajzen's theory of planned behaviour (Ajzen, 1991).

developed an ingrained negative attitude towards academic learning because of their past experiences, attend a school where apathy or disruption amongst the students with learning difficulties is the norm, and if they feel a sense of learned helplessness because they do not feel any sense of personal control, then no amount of intensive instruction, however skilled, is likely to make much difference in terms of long-term learning outcomes.

(b) The self

The basic tenets of self theory have been described in the previous chapter. The main point to be re-emphasized here is that dyslexia reveals itself as fundamentally an educational issue which is likely to affect the individual's academic self-concept in the first instance. This in turn will influence the development of a sense of identity as a learner and, thereby, the individual's feelings of self-esteem. What we need to know, therefore, is how the dyslexic individual currently perceives him/herself as a learner and problem-solver, and how this academic self-concept was shaped as a result of that individual's learning career.

(c) Sense of agency

In many respects a person's self-esteem can be seen to be closely related to their sense of agency in that the degree to which we value ourselves with regard to any activity will depend in large part upon how competent we think we are, how confident we are in performing well when required to do so, how much in control of the outcomes we consider ourselves to be, the ways in which we react to disappointment and failure, the strategies that we have at our disposal and the amount of effort we are prepared to invest in order to succeed.

In attempting to assess self-esteem, therefore, we need to explore these aspects of the individual's sense of agency. In particular, we can benefit considerably by focusing on aspects of self-efficacy and locus of control on the one hand, and learned helplessness and depression on the other.

Self-efficacy

This term was first introduced by Albert Bandura in the 1970s as a central aspect of his social cognitive theory of human behaviour (Bandura, 1986). He has continued to update his theory as new research findings have emerged, until the publication in 1997 of *Self-efficacy: The Exercise of Control*, in which he situated self-efficacy within a theory of personal and collective agency that operates in conjunction with other socio-cognitive factors in regulating human well-being and attainment. According to this theory individuals possess a self-system that enables them to exercise a measure of control over their thoughts, feelings, motivations and actions (Pajares, 1999). Thus our behaviour is seen as very much under the control of what we believe we are capable of achieving. It is not enough, therefore, to possess knowledge and/or skills in order to be successful, we also have to believe that we can use these attributes to our best advantage.

Locus of control (LOC)

A central aspect of both self-efficacy theory and attribution theory is locus of control, a term derived from the social learning theory of Rotter (1954), which refers to a person's beliefs about their control over life events. Some people, termed 'internalizers', feel personally responsible for everything that happens to them, whilst others, termed 'externalizers', feel that their outcomes in life are determined by forces beyond their control, e.g. by fate, luck or other people.

Whilst most people fall somewhere between these extremes, there is considerable evidence to suggest that many tend towards one end of the continuum or the other where significant life events are concerned. The situation is somewhat more complicated in that people can often vary in how far they feel in control over negative as opposed to positive events in their lives. There are some indications, for example, that males tend to attribute positive outcomes to internal causes and negative outcomes to external causes, whereas the reverse tends to be true of females.

From their extensive review of research studies into the relationship between LOC and academic achievement, Findley and Cooper (1983) were able to conclude that more internal beliefs are associated with higher achievement. The relationship tends to be stronger for males than females and appears to apply across ethnic groups. Other significant findings are that externalizers tend to exhibit less persistence in tasks, whereas internalizers show a greater willingness to delay rewards in order to maximize them and tend to prefer situations involving skill rather than chance.

One of the most significant educational intervention programmes built upon the locus of control construct was developed by de Charms (1976), who was able to show that programmes designed to teach teachers how to help children take on a greater sense of personal responsibility and power with regard to their academic futures can have a positive effect on those children's future achievements. We can therefore predict that there will be a strong positive relationship between the feelings of internal locus of control held by those with dyslexic difficulties and their likelihood of success in overcoming their difficulties.

An important implication of self-efficacy theory is that people's behaviour can often be predicted better by their beliefs about their capabilities than by what they know or by how they may have behaved on a previous occasion. This does not mean that knowledge and skills are not important or that we can achieve beyond the level of our capabilities just by believing that we can, rather that our beliefs about our capabilities help determine what we do with them. In school, for example, the beliefs that students develop about their capabilities help to determine what they do with the knowledge they have acquired. Two students with the same level of ability or past accomplishment may well differ in their ultimate educational achievements as a result of what they believe they are capable of achieving.

Bandura describes self-efficacy beliefs as 'beliefs in one's capability to organise and execute the courses of action required to manage prospective situations' (1997, p. 2).

In this respect, self-efficacy beliefs are usually considered to be more contextualized – more task or situation specific – than other theories relating to more generalized feelings of self-competence. Self-efficacy theory should therefore be seen as one aspect of more general motivation or self-concept theory. It is concerned with feelings of *agency* in specific circumstances.

The most influential source of self-efficacy information is considered to be a person's past *mastery experience*. If we interpret the effect of our actions as having been previously successful, we will be more likely to believe that similar actions will lead to success on a future occasion, but the three-way link between capability, action and belief is crucial. It will not be enough, therefore, when working to help people overcome their learning difficulties, to improve competence or feeling of self-worth alone; there must also be an improved understanding of how the application of knowledge or skill leads to successful outcomes together with a belief in one's own capability in making that application.

Two other important sources of self-efficacy information are the *vicarious experiences* that we have as a result of the actions of others, particularly significant others in our lives, and the *verbal persuasions* that we receive from those others. It has been suggested (Schunk, 1983) that this makes the existence of role or peer models particularly important in our lives in instilling the self-beliefs that will influence the course and direction that life will take. Making comparisons with peer models can also have a negative effect if it leads us to believe that we are less capable of achieving than our peers. The evidence would seem to suggest, moreover, that it is easier to weaken self-efficacy beliefs through negative appraisals by significant others than to strengthen these beliefs through positive encouragement (Bandura, 1986).

Self-efficacy beliefs are considered to affect motivation and self-regulation in a number of ways (Pajares, 1999). They influence the *choices* we make in deciding whether or how to act, the amount of *effort* we are prepared to invest in any activity, how long we *persevere* when confronted by obstacles, our level of *resilience* in the face of adversity and even the amount of *stress* and *anxiety* we feel when engaged in any task. Thus, if we have a strong sense of self-competence in any particular academic area we will be more likely to see tasks set in that area as challenges to be mastered rather than threats to be avoided, we are likely to have greater intrinsic interest in the activities, to set ourselves challenging goals and maintain a strong commitment to them, increase our efforts when faced with failure and more easily recover our confidence after a setback.

There is now considerable research evidence to support Bandura's contention that self-efficacy beliefs mediate the effect of skills or other self-beliefs on attainments in educational and work settings (Bandura, 1997; Schunk, 1991; Zimmerman, 1995). Much of this research has been carried out with regard to mathematics attainment. For example, Schunk (1984) reported that mathematics self-efficacy influenced performance on mathematics tasks both directly and indirectly through persistence. As yet less work has been done on the relationship between self-efficacy and literacy accomplishment. The potential implications for dyslexic students are not difficult to see, however, as also are the links with learned helplessness theory. Dyslexics, by definition, suffer mainly from specific learning difficulties in specific domains, most usually literacy. The very specific nature of their difficulties indicates that they are capable of learning, often extremely well, in other areas. Much of the specialist help they are given to overcome their difficulties is based upon skills training of one kind or another. Such skills training is sometimes, but not always, accompanied by efforts to boost their self-esteem. What self-efficacy theory suggests is that academically unsuccessful dyslexics are likely to be lacking in confidence about their capabilities for becoming successfully literate, will choose to avoid tasks involving reading and/or writing, will be inclined to expend less effort on such tasks, to lack resilience, and to be more vulnerable to stress and anxiety in academic situations. Moreover, if they are to overcome their difficulties, they will need help in developing not only new skills and strategies but also a sense of agency whereby their belief in their ability to apply their newly learnt skills is strong enough to overcome the obstacles they will continue to meet.

Learned helplessness

The theory of learned helplessness was first formulated by Martin Seligman and his colleagues in the 1970s following experimental work with animals who were unable to avoid the consequences of uncontrollable shock. The key text, *Helplessness: On Depression Development and Death*, published in 1975, reported the generalization of the negative influence on problem-solving behaviour of uncontrollable trauma or insoluble problems together with the similarities in emotional reactions to those suffering from depression. A number of subsequent studies provided confirmatory evidence of these findings. However, continuing dispute about the interpretation of the findings led to a reformulation of the theory more in line with Rotter's social learning theory and Weiner's attribution theory (Gilbert, 1992).

The reformulated theory of learned helplessness by Abramson, Seligman and Teasdale in 1978 stressed the three central aspects of attribution theory – whether a person's actions were internally perceived as (a) controlled by internal or external forces (locus of causality/control), (b) stable or unstable/changeable, (c) global/general or task/activity specific. Attribution theory suggests that the reasons we attribute to perceived successes and failures in our lives can have a profound influence upon our subsequent actions. If we see events as being mainly within our own control, as being open to change and as being specific rather than representative of life in general, then we are more likely to feel capable of dealing with those events in a positive manner as they arise. If, on the other hand, we feel that what happens to us is outside our control, unchangeable and global rather than specific, we will come to consider that nothing we do will work, and give up trying. This, in turn, can lead to feelings of depression. As Gilbert explains,

> The severity and chronicity of depression are in part the result of the perceived cause of not being able to control desired outcomes. Internal, personal, stable attributions will lead the individual to believe that the failure to control an outcome is due to deficits within themselves and that the same state of affairs will remain in the future. In this way, the chosen dimension of attribution will lead to both a fall in self-esteem and a hopeless view of the future. (Gilbert, 1992, p. 371).

Seligman and his colleagues have shown that depressed college students tend to attribute negative outcomes to more internal, stable and global causes than non-depressed students (Seligman et al., 1979). Thus a depressed dyslexic would be more likely to see their problems as being due to their own general stupidity, which could not be changed. A more positive scenario would be one where the dyslexic took an internal, changeable and specific attitude to learning, i.e. they viewed themselves as personally responsible for their current failures which were only in specific aspects of their learning, and capable of improvement, given a positive approach and appropriate help, as is illustrated in Table 2.2.

Table 2.2 The dyslexic child's possible internal attributions for learning failure

	Stable	Unstable/Changeable
Global	I am a poor learner	I am sometimes a poor learner, but I can get better
	I am stupid	I sometimes feel stupid but not always/most of the time
	I am useless	I sometimes feel useless but at other times I feel capable of achieving success
Specific	I find some aspects of school work impossible to learn	I can learn these things if I'm taught in the right way
	I am hopeless at some lessons	I sometimes feel hopeless in certain lessons, but not all of the time
	I will never learn to read or spell	I can't read or spell very well but I can improve with help

There would appear to be growing evidence that attribution retraining of this nature can have a positive effect on both the achievements and motivation of children with learning disabilities (Borkowski et al., 1988; Craske, 1988; Van Overwalle and de Metsenaere, 1990).

Depression

Depression is a highly complex area about which there has been considerable disagreement between experts from different professional backgrounds. For many years it was considered unlikely by some that children could suffer from depression. However, the current general consensus is that at least 4% of the adolescent population may show signs of major depression and that this can have adverse effects on both development and attainments, which may well carry over into adult life (Gilbert, 1992). One of the main difficulties for those seeking to find methods for early identification and treatment is to differentiate between so-called endogenous depression of biological origin and exogenous depression which is caused by social circumstances or negative life events. In some circumstances the two conditions may well be interactive rather than mutually exclusive.

Gilbert suggests that one helpful theoretical explanation for some exogenous depression is that of social ranking. In his words (1992, p. 150), 'there is a natural tendency to understand, think about or construe relationships, between things, people and objects, in terms of some ranked relationship, and these constructions influence our attention and behaviour towards them'. If we see ourselves as negatively ranked with regard to a highly valued activity in comparison with our peers, and particularly if we can see no way of altering our status in this respect, then the likelihood of feelings of depression is considerably increased.

The connection between learned helplessness and depression is made by Seligman in the following way: 'A pessimistic explanatory style is at the core of depressed thinking. A negative concept of the future, the self, and the world stems from seeing the causes of bad events as permanent, pervasive, and personal, and seeing the causes of good events in the opposite way' (1991, p. 58). In other words (p. 54), 'Depression is pessimism writ large'.

It should be apparent from this that there are natural links between depression and learned helplessness, with the former representing a potential extreme outcome of the latter. Gilbert makes clear these associations by pointing out that both sets of theories focus on a perceived sense of defeat and uncontrollability of outcomes, but ranking theory places a greater emphasis on the social context within which such negative self-evaluations develop.

There is considerable research to show that depression in adults is related to various aspects of people's perceptions of themselves such as feelings of being inadequate and a failure, and having a tendency to attribute negative outcomes to oneself whilst attributing positive outcomes to forces outside one's control (Abramson et al., 1978). Research on the development of depressive tendencies in childhood has tended to support the hypothesis that repeated negative experiences during the childhood years can and often do play a significant part in this. Early indications would appear to be a poor self-concept and negatively expressed beliefs about the reasons for performing poorly at school, together with a lack of confidence to bring about positive change (Murray et al., 2001). A further study by Bandura and colleagues (1999) found a significant negative relationship between children's feelings of social and academic efficacy and levels of depression, academic achievement and problem behaviour.

The potential implications of these ideas and findings for dyslexics are self-evident. In most societies children grow up in an educational environment in which literacy and numeracy are considered essential prerequisites for any form of academic achievement. Failure to develop these foundation skills will almost inevitably position a person low down in the educational ranks, no matter what other positive attributes they may possess. Indeed, the more intelligent that person may otherwise prove to be, the more likely they are to be aware of their scholastic shortcomings. If they are also unable to overcome their early difficulties, no matter how hard they try, the greater the likelihood of descent into feelings of learned helplessness and, ultimately, depression. As we saw in the previous chapter, the little research that currently exists into the connection between dyslexia and low self-esteem, learned helplessness and depression has tended to confirm this hypothesis.

The importance of explanatory style

Seligman has described learned helplessness as 'the giving up reaction, the quitting response that follows from the belief that whatever you do doesn't matter'. He came to see this as one possible outcome of what he terms people's 'explanatory style', which he defines as 'the manner in which you habitually explain to yourself why events happen. It is the great modulator of learned helplessness. An optimistic explanatory style stops helplessness, whereas a pessimistic explanatory style spreads helplessness' (1991, p. 15).

In the same text (1991, p. 67), Seligman goes on to argue that neither learned helplessness nor depression need be permanent states or explanatory styles. 'Learned helplessness (can) be cured by showing the subject his own actions (will) now work. It (can) also be cured by teaching the subject to think differently about what caused him to fail.'

Unresolved dilemmas

The question remains as to whether difficulties of a dyslexic nature must inevitably be accompanied by feelings of learned helplessness and low self-efficacy. Why and how do many children with dyslexia become depressed and lapse into feelings of learned helplessness by early adolescence? If and when they do, are they doomed to a future of failure or can something be done to help them develop a sense of agency where they see the likelihood of a positive future lying in their own hands? In order to begin to find answers to such questions we first need to avail ourselves of suitable assessment techniques for measuring development and change in the key areas that have been identified.

Our exploration of the nature of the self-concept has highlighted its complexity, particularly with regard to its multi-faceted nature, the often confusing and overlapping use of terms and the difficulties associated with identifying appropriate forms of measurement. We cannot always be certain, therefore, whether researchers using the same terms are necessarily measuring the same phenomenon or even whether those using very different terms are not referring to the same thing. Hansford and Hattie (1982) provide a helpful meta-analysis of self-concept research which highlights many of these difficulties. This led us to the decision not to focus in our research on any of the more commonly used techniques for measuring self-concept or self-esteem. Instead we decided to employ a more *triangulated* approach within which we identified what we considered to be key aspects of the ways that individuals' personal constructions of themselves as learners relate to the actual process of learning.

With this in mind, the themes of young people's perceptions of themselves as learners and problem-solvers, their feelings of self-efficacy and internal locus of control as compared with a sense of learned helplessness and even depression were indicated as most likely to be significant to a socio-cultural perspective on learning. This also made it essential that we contextualized our research within the personal and collective histories of dyslexic individuals.

One of our primary tasks, therefore, has been to construct appropriate theory-based instruments which are capable of illuminating these issues. The identification and construction of such instruments will be described in the next chapter.

CHAPTER 3

Approaches to assessment

We decided upon a multi-faceted approach to assessment which incorporated four main features:

1. a semi-structured interview
2. a measure of academic self-concept (Myself-as-a-Learner Scale)
3. a measure of dyslexics' sense of agency (Dyslexia Identity Scale)
4. a set of sentence completion items.

Interview

A semi-structured, in-depth interview schedule was constructed which focused on such issues as a brief family description, a personalized description of the current major areas of difficulty, an account of the child's earliest memories of realizing there was a problem and the reactions of significant others to this, the process of formal diagnosis and its consequences, and a comparison between the educational regimes of the current and previous schools. This schedule and the way in which it was employed is described below.

Interview schedule for dyslexic students

The interview is always begun with a personal introduction to the interviewer and a few details about their background including a brief explanation about the purpose of the research. This explanation is followed by a genuine invitation to the interviewee to participate *or not*. This is both for ethical reasons and because it is important to obtain open, honest, willing contributions to the interviews, thereby contributing to the validity of the outcome data.

This invitation usually takes the form of the following words:

I/we am/are really interested in finding out what it feels like to be dyslexic (have specific learning difficulties) because there has been a great deal written about dyslexia (SpLD) but very few people have asked dyslexics themselves what it is like. If you are interested, I/we would like to ask you some questions about the sort of things that have happened to you during your school career, how you found out you were dyslexic, the people who have helped you or not, how you are feeling now, and things like that.

I/we'd also like you to tell me/us honestly what you think about this school – what are its good and not so good points – and maybe how things could be improved.

What you tell me/us will be in complete confidence, but I/we'll be collecting together the views of everyone I/we interview and writing them up in a book and/or research paper.

You really don't have to take part if you don't want to, but I/we would really value your opinion and would like to hear your story if you'd like to tell me/us.

If the student agrees to participate, the interview then begins with the collection of such demographic data as name, age, position in family, father's/mother's occupation, other family details (e.g. familial history of dyslexia), residence, time spent in present school, number and location of previous schools.

The questions in the semi-structured interview schedule which follows do not always have to be asked in the same order, but can be woven into a more conversational style with further probing at various points if only brief or unclear answers are forthcoming.

Interview questions

- What does the word 'dyslexic' mean to you? (The term SpLD may be used alternatively in some mainstream schools.)
- Can you have different kinds of dyslexia?
- If so, what kind are you?
- Is some people's dyslexia more severe than others'?
- If so, how severe is yours?
- What are your main difficulties?
- Do you have difficulties in subjects other than English? Why do you think that is?
- How do people come to be dyslexic? Born like it . . . etc.?
- Can dyslexia be cured?

- If so, how? If not, can you get better in any way? If so, how?
- How old were you when you first found out you were dyslexic?
- How did it happen? Who told (diagnosed) you?
- What had happened before then? How did teachers/other kids react to you?
- How did you feel when you were told? Did you understand what it meant? If not, how did you find out? (Parents' views?)
- Do you think you fully understand it now?
- Do you tell other people about it or keep it to yourself? Do you think they understand?
- What happened after you were diagnosed? Did anything change? Did things get better? If not, why not?
- Who has helped you most to understand and come to terms with your dyslexia? How did they do that?
- Why was it decided that you should transfer to this school? Did you have any say in the matter? Did you want to transfer?
- What would have helped you cope in a mainstream school – what could anyone have done to make things work for you there? Would you rather have gone to a different school?
- Why do you think it didn't work for you?
- What are the main differences between this school and your previous school(s) in helping you overcome your dyslexic difficulties?
- Do you think you miss anything by coming to a boarding special school (where relevant)?
- How does it feel to be labelled dyslexic? Relieved, ashamed . . . ?
- Does being dyslexic have anything good about it?
- What do you think the future holds . . . ambitions?

Academic self-concept

This was assessed by means of a standardized scale (the Myself-as-a-Learner Scale; Burden, 2000b) specifically designed to assess young people's perceptions of themselves as learners and problem-solvers within the academic context.

This scale was originally constructed to meet a perceived gap in resources for assessing the ways in which children in their middle and secondary school years constructed an image of themselves as learners and problem-solvers. Despite the fact that there have been literally hundreds of studies demonstrating the positive relationship between self-concept and achievement, the complex nature of this relationship allied to problems of measurement has left a number of important questions unanswered. Most measurement scales have been the products of researchers in the USA who have attempted to take into account the multi-faceted nature of people's self-perceptions (see Byrne, 1996, for an excellent overview of such techniques).

Self-concept measurement scales of this kind have usually identified five or six key areas and produced a number of items relating to these areas, the responses to which are added together to give a general self-concept (GSC) score or are presented as a profile of different subscale scores. The advantages of such scales are that they are comprehensive, well standardized (though not usually in the UK) and widely used. There is often, but not always, strong statistical evidence of validity and reliability. Their disadvantages are that they tend to be long and time-consuming to administer, score and interpret, particularly when used with children with literacy difficulties, and may contain only relatively few items devoted specifically to a person's learning self-concept. This last point is important because research has shown that the strongest association with academic achievement is with learning/academic self-concept (ASC) rather than general self-concept (GSC) (Hansford and Hattie, 1982).

An alternative approach, therefore, is to construct measurement scales that focus specifically on one or other aspect of self-concept such as body image, perceived sporting ability, learning self-concept or, even more specifically, ability in reading or mathematics. This approach has the advantage of producing briefer and more focused scales, which tend to be easier to administer and score, but which lay no claim to providing information about a respondent's more general self-concept or any other aspect of it.

Somewhat surprisingly, few scales exist that focus specifically on learning self-concept. With this in mind, the Myself-as-a-Learner Scale (MALS) was constructed to meet a perceived need for a scale that was moderately but not too brief, easy to read and comprehend, and straightforward to score and interpret. A pilot study reduced the original 40 items to 20 statements such as 'I know how to solve the problems that I meet', 'When I'm given new work to do, I usually feel confident I can do it' and 'Learning is difficult'. Respondents are required to indicate on a five-point scale whether they agree strongly, agree somewhat, aren't quite sure, disagree somewhat or disagree strongly with each statement. A resultant overall score out of 100 can be compared with standardized norms to identify any individual's level of academic self-concept, but the scale can also be used to identify specific patterns of response indicating perceived strengths and weaknesses.

Standardization of the MALS was initially carried out on 389 secondary school students between the ages of 11 and 13, but subsequent studies have shown it to be valid when used with adults and with children as young as 9. Factor analysis showed it to have a robust factor structure, and a strong alpha correlation of 0.84 attests to its internal consistency. Significant positive correlations were found with verbal reasoning scores (0.41), non-verbal reasoning (0.35), reading (0.38) and mathematics (0.34) test scores. Full details about the construction and use of the scale can be found in Burden (1998, 2000b).

Sense of agency

This was investigated by means of a specially constructed, theory-based questionnaire entitled the Dyslexia Identity Scale (DIS). The purpose of this 25-item scale is to elicit the feelings of children and adults with dyslexic difficulties about being understood by others, about whether they felt confident and in control of their future learning outcomes, or whether, by contrast, they felt helpless to improve and even depressed because of this. The content of the DIS (Box 3.1), together with instructions for its administration and scoring protocols, is described below.

The Dyslexia Identity Scale (DIS)

The DIS has been constructed as an aid in the exploration of the developing sense of identity of children and young people prior to and following their identification as displaying specific learning difficulties of a dyslexic nature. It is based on the premise that the thoughts and feelings people have about their ability to learn and to be successful at various life tasks will act as important mediating variables between their actual measured abilities and ultimate success in those tasks. In particular, the psychological concepts of self-efficacy, locus of control and learned helplessness are drawn upon to illuminate those feelings.

Self-efficacy represents a person's feelings of competence and confidence of success when faced with specific learning and/or assessment tasks. At a more general level it also reflects a person's sense of their general ability to cope and perform well academically.

Locus of control refers to the beliefs that people hold about whether the things that happen to them in their lives are mainly within their own control or at the mercy of other people or outside forces.

Learned helplessness reflects the ingrained sense of failure and inability to succeed that some people carry with them as a result of continual negative experiences in academic or more general aspects of their lives. In its most extreme form this can lead to attendant feelings of *depression*.

Within the DIS each of these factors is assessed by means of rating statements along a five-point scale whereby respondents are required to indicate whether the statements are definitely true (YES), somewhat true (yes), not very true (no), definitely not true (NO), or whether they are just not sure (?). Scores on each item are then accumulated for each subscale and a personal (or group) profile is constructed, which is best used in conjunction with information gathered from interviews and other sources.

The DIS also provides information on the level of *understanding* that the dyslexic student considers other people to show about his or her condition and whether that understanding has grown or diminished as a result of changing circumstances such as their transfer from one school to another. This aspect of the scale is administered in the same way as the others, but the results are not treated in a cumulative manner.

Box 3.1 The Dyslexia Identity Scale

The following statements are about how it feels to be dyslexic. Every dyslexic person feels differently. We want to know exactly how you feel. There are no right or wrong answers so please be as honest as you can. All you have to do is read or listen to each statement and then draw a circle around YES, yes, ?, no, NO. If you think the statement is **definitely true**, please circle 'YES'. If you think it's **quite true**, please circle 'yes'. If you're **not sure** or it's **sometimes true** and sometimes not true, please circle '?'. If you think it's not **usually true**, please circle 'no'. If it's **definitely not true**, please circle 'NO'.

1.	Most people understand how it feels to be dyslexic	YES	yes	?	no	NO
2.	The teachers at my last school really understood my difficulties	YES	yes	?	no	NO
3.	I wish I wasn't dyslexic	YES	yes	?	no	NO
4.	If I try hard I can achieve as much as anyone else	YES	yes	?	no	NO
5.	Being dyslexic really bothers me	YES	yes	?	no	NO
6.	I can be good at maths if I really want to	YES	yes	?	no	NO

7.	My dyslexia makes it impossible for me to do really well at school	YES	yes	?	no	NO
8.	I can be good at English if I really want to	YES	yes	?	no	NO
9.	Before I came to this school I used to feel depressed about being dyslexic	YES	yes	?	no	NO
10.	The teachers at this school really understand my difficulties	YES	yes	?	no	NO
11.	I have the ability to do well in exams if I want to	YES	yes	?	no	NO
12.	Dyslexia is a curse	YES	yes	?	no	NO
13.	On the whole I feel good about myself	YES	yes	?	no	NO
14.	There are a lot worse things than being dyslexic	YES	yes	?	no	NO
15.	However hard I try, I'll never be as good at school work as someone who isn't dyslexic	YES	yes	?	no	NO
16.	I keep wishing my dyslexia would go away	YES	yes	?	no	NO
17.	Only another dyslexic person can really understand how it feels to be dyslexic	YES	yes	?	no	NO
18.	A lot of the time I feel depressed about being dyslexic	YES	yes	?	no	NO
19.	How well I do in the future is up to me	YES	yes	?	no	NO
20.	I will always be held back by my dyslexic difficulties	YES	yes	?	no	NO
21.	My mother understands how I feel about being dyslexic	YES	yes	?	no	NO
22.	My father understands how I feel about being dyslexic	YES	yes	?	no	NO
23.	I have made a lot of progress since coming to this school	YES	yes	?	no	NO
24.	I know how I can overcome my learning difficulties	YES	yes	?	no	NO
25.	Most of the time I like being me	YES	yes	?	no	NO

Thematic indicators

(a) Self-efficacy/locus of control items

4. If I try hard I can achieve as much as anyone else
6. I can be good at Maths if I really want to
8. I can be good at English if I really want to
11. I have the ability to do well in exams if I want to
19. How well I do in the future is up to me
24. I know how I can overcome my learning difficulties

Highest possible score: 30
Lowest possible score: 6
Positive self-efficacy indicated by a score of 20 or above

(b) Learned helplessness items

7. My dyslexia makes it impossible for me to do really well at school
15. However hard I try, I'll never be as good at school work as some-one who isn't dyslexic
20. I will always be held back by my dyslexic difficulties

Highest possible score: 15
Lowest possible score: 3
Learned helplessness indicated by a score of 10 or above

(c) Depression items

3. I wish I wasn't dyslexic
5. Being dyslexic really bothers me
9. Before I came to this school I used to feel depressed about being dyslexic
12. Dyslexia is a curse
16. I keep wishing my dyslexia would go away
18. A lot of the time I feel depressed about being dyslexic

Highest possible score: 30
Lowest possible score: 6
Possible depression indicated by a score of 20 or above

(d) Feelings of being understood

1. Most people understand how it feels to be dyslexic
2. The teachers at my last school really understood my difficulties
10. The teachers at this school really understand my difficulties
17. Only another dyslexic person can really understand how it feels to be dyslexic
21. My mother understands how I feel about being dyslexic
22. My father understands how I feel about being dyslexic

Identity profile

Self-efficacy/Locus of control score: Indications:

Learned helplessness score: Indications:

Depression score: Indications:

Feelings of being understood: Indications:

Summary of key points emerging from
each aspect of the identity profile:

Further self-concept items

Finally, an open-ended sentence-completion instrument was devised which covered some of the same ground as that in the interview schedule, partly as a means of checking the consistency of the interviewees' responses. Extra items also allowed for a little more probing into the respondents' current subject preferences and attributions for success and failure. This instrument took the form shown in Box 3.2.

Box 3.2 The 'All about me' instrument

I am going to read to you the first part of some unfinished sentences. What I'd like you to do is to finish each sentence off for me with the first thoughts that come into your head. Don't stop to think too much about your answers, just try to let the words come out for themselves.

1. My name is . . .

2. My birthday is . . .

3. My favourite food is . . .

4. My favourite pastime (hobby) is . . .

5. When I leave school I want to . . .

6. The things I like best about this school are . . .

7. The things I don't like so much are . . .

8. My favourite subjects are . . .

9. I like them because . . .

10. The subjects I don't like much are . . .

11. I don't like them because . . .

12. When I do well at my schoolwork, the main reasons are usually because . . .

13. When I don't do so well at my schoolwork, the main reasons are usually because . . .

14. A good thing about being me is . . . because . . .

15. A not-so-good thing about being me is . . . because . . .

16. I feel really happy when . . .

17. I feel miserable when . . .

18. The best thing that has ever happened to me was . . .

19. The worst thing about being dyslexic is . . .

20. The ways I have been helped most are . . .

21. I get annoyed when . . .

22. The thing I need most now is . . .

23. Dyslexia . . .

24. If I wanted to help someone else understand their dyslexia, I would tell them . . .

Trialling the assessment techniques

The opportunity was made available to interview 50 adolescent boys, who made up a significant proportion (60%) of the boys attending an independent specialist residential school for dyslexics between the ages of 11 and 16 situated within the West of England. Permission was first obtained from the boys' parents, and subsequently from the boys themselves, to carry out the interviews, each of which lasted about 45 minutes. All the interviews were completed within the space of 8 weeks.

This is clearly not a random sample of typical dyslexic adolescents. In some respects, however, its very specialized nature provides us with considerable advantages. We can be sure, for example, that every participant is dyslexic, at least with regard to criteria specified by the school. They had all had to demonstrate evidence of at least average intelligence on standardized testing whilst at the same time manifesting considerable difficulties in establishing literacy (or in some cases, numeracy), with no evidence of marked emotional or behavioural difficulties. They were therefore, by definition, academically underachieving at the point of their entry to the school.

It can be seen therefore that in this instance the implicit definition of dyslexia that was being employed by the school was one relating to the discrepancy between IQ or manifest general cognitive abilities and lower than expected attainments in literacy and/or numeracy. This is not to say that the educators involved considered this to be the only or even most helpful definition of dyslexia, but it is one they felt best met the demands of the examination-oriented curriculum to which the school was geared.

From a research point of view, this made the interviewing task much easier to carry out than might otherwise have been the case and in most instances ensured that the boys could describe quite clearly, and often passionately, their early educational experiences and their personal reactions to them.

The following chapter provides a thematic analysis of the boys' personal histories in the development of their sense of identity as a dyslexic person.

CHAPTER 4

Learning careers as foundations for the formation of a dyslexic identity

When we analysed the personal histories of our 50 dyslexic boys we found that a number of significant themes began to emerge. These themes fitted together to form a coherent pattern which we have chosen to describe as their constructions of their *learning careers*, a concept that emphasizes the notion of learning as a *process* rather than a set of outcomes. In this it can be seen as a precursor to what Pollard (1996) terms children's 'learning stance', i.e. the characteristic approach they adopt when confronted by a new learning challenge. In his words, 'A child's learning stance is clearly linked to their sense of identity and to the self-confidence which they generate from available cultural resources, social expectations and personal awareness of potential' (Pollard, 1996, p. 10).

For Pollard this learning stance is shaped by the opportunities and risks that exist for each child to learn within different social settings, incorporating the power relations and social expectations within which they must act and adapt. The learning challenges themselves are provided by the experiences, relationships and tasks that occur within the main settings of home, playground and classroom. Thus a child's learning career, which is a major contributor to the establishment of his or her learning stance, incorporates the challenges with which they have been faced and the help or hindrances provided by significant others in meeting these challenges.

Each of the significant themes running through the boys' learning careers will now be described in turn.

Confusion

Many of the boys' earliest memories of school were of feeling confused and frustrated at their inability to master tasks that others, often with less evident abilities, seemed able to manage quite easily. This sense of confusion, which often led to a feeling of not quite 'belonging' and sometimes even alienation, is illustrated in the following quotes.

Charles (13 years 6 months: Year 8)

All my friends were reading and I couldn't. It took me nearly 3 years to read *The Twits* or something. They were all reading really well and I got a bit upset by them all reading and I wasn't. It didn't affect my behaviour, I just got a bit upset about it and then the teacher sometimes told me off because I'm not reading or I didn't understand what they were talking about and my mum looked for (other) schools ...

Martin (14 years 3 months: Year 9)

The first school I can remember going to I was always behind. I couldn't catch up. I always needed help. I went to a special class in that school. It didn't feel very nice because I never got help and I was always behind everyone else and I couldn't catch up. The other kids didn't treat me differently, but I just felt that I wasn't part of the class.

It would seem that a primary task for all dyslexics, if they are ever to overcome the emotional consequences related to their learning difficulties, is to work through this confusion and make personal sense of why those difficulties are occurring. This is one reason why early identification and diagnosis is so important, particularly in the way in which the diagnosis is explained to the young person concerned.

The following quotes demonstrate that the boys in our sample found different ways of working through this confusion, almost always with the help of a significant adult, usually one or both parents or a teacher.

Keith (12 years 8 months: Year 7)

I was found out to be dyslexic in Year 4. My mum always thought I was dyslexic 'cos she's been a teacher. She told the infants school but they did not do anything about it, so we moved. The next school listened and they did something about it. I saw an educational psychologist and did some tests. She said I was intelligent but I needed help with my writing and I needed computers.

Tom (13 years 9 months: Year 8)

My mum thought I was dyslexic for ages, so I went to this tutor. She said I was nowhere near dyslexic, I was just dumb. So we had about 10 more tests and everyone else said I was dumb. Then I went up to the dyslexic place in Bristol and they said 'How can anybody miss it?' That was in Year 7, last year before Christmas.

Jonathan (14 years 6 months: Year 10)

When I was in Year 3 my teacher mentioned I might be dyslexic, that's why I might be struggling. Then I had this test with a psychologist and then with the teacher who used to help me. I just felt . . . I kind of blamed it on me. I felt I must try harder. You're not trying hard enough, it's all your fault. Once I was kind of diagnosed. I got rid of it. It wasn't a major thing.

Seeking to resolve the confusion: the value of metaphor

When we are confused about things that happen to us in our lives, each of us tries to make sense of what is happening in our own individual ways, often by conjuring up a picture in our minds of the problems with which we are faced in order to make them more real and/or manageable. This use of language and non-verbal images to represent an idea or concept in another way is what we mean by metaphor.

The importance of the use of metaphor has become increasing recognized by psychologists as a way of revealing the deeper roots of people's ways of looking at the world. Leary (1999) even suggests that all knowledge is ultimately rooted in metaphorical modes of perception or thought and that self-consciousness must therefore necessarily result from metaphorical thinking. He considers this to be particularly true for those aspects of our experience that we have not quite been able to make sense of in our conscious minds.

In the words of Ozik (1986, p. 67), 'metaphor transforms the strange into the familiar'. Moreover for Black (1979, p. 37) 'a metaphorical statement can sometimes generate new knowledge and insight by changing the relationships between the things designated'. He goes on to suggest (p. 39) that 'some metaphors enable us to see aspects of reality that the metaphor's production helps to constitute'. A similar view is expressed by Sfard (1998), who contends that the use of different metaphors may lead to different ways of thinking and acting. She goes on to suggest that one way to explore fundamental, primary levels of thinking about learning is to 'dig out' the metaphors underlying our spontaneous everyday conceptions and scientific theorizing because, she argues, they have a special power to enable us to cross the borders between the spontaneous and the scientific.

Accessing the metaphors of dyslexics

We decided that a helpful way of drawing upon these ideas would be to explore with dyslexic young people the metaphors that they had constructed for themselves, or were able to construct with supportive prompting, to make sense of their dyslexic condition. We felt also that such metaphors might well provide some hidden indication of the ways in which dyslexic individuals had resolved their confusion and would be most likely to act in dealing with the difficulties they faced.

As part of our Dyslexia Interview Schedule we therefore included the following question:

> If you were to imagine dyslexia as some kind of 'thing' or picture in your mind, how would you describe it?

This question generated a surprisingly wide range of metaphors from the students, most of whom responded with enthusiasm to the request. These responses were then analysed by means of a process of 'iterative analysis' (Huberman and Miles, 1994), which made it possible to construct several different overarching categories. The majority of the metaphors related to some form of obstacle or barrier that was interfering with the learning process, but these could fairly readily be divided into those that were considered surmountable by means of some form of extra effort or strategy, and those that appeared insurmountable.

Surmountable barriers

Most of the metaphors generated in this category tended to describe dyslexia in terms of barriers that needed to be, and indeed could be, surmounted. This reflected the high sense of internal locus of control and lack of feelings of learned helplessness demonstrated by the majority of the students throughout the interview process.

Sometimes these metaphors took a relatively simple form.

> A wall with paths going round it.

At other times they were more lucidly explicit in describing action that needed to be taken.

> It's like a lock and key. If you've got enough persistence you can sort of find that key to unlock that door. If you keep doing it, you keep unlocking all

the doors, so eventually you get to the end passage, It's like a maze with doors that you've got to unlock, so you have to keep persisting.

It is perhaps unsurprising that this student demonstrated in several other ways an extremely high level of internal locus of control and no feelings of learned helplessness.

Sometimes the metaphors categorized as demonstrating barriers that could be surmounted were more obscure and usually graphic, but each can be seen as representing some form of positive outlook.

It's a big blob of something sticky – it, like, sticks to you. You can't get rid of it really, but you can get rid of little bits.

Or, even more graphically,

I think it's like an onion. It's got lots of different layers. One layer may be good and one layer may be, like, half there, and one might not be. And, say, if you put a layer on, it would, like, peel off, kind of thing. And you'd have to stick it back on with, like, Pritt Stick, and, like, hold it there a while to make sure it stays.

Another form of metaphor in this category took a more *skills development* perspective.

It's like when toddlers are crawling and then they start to walk. Then they're slow on their feet, but as they get older they learn how to run.

An enthusiastic and hard-working boy who was very keen on team sports described his own very appropriate metaphor:

Not being able to make a (rugby) tackle or something like that. When you miss a tackle, you feel disappointed in yourself. That's how I feel about spelling and that. When I can't get something into my head I feel disappointed, and then when somebody tells you it, you get it back.

Insurmountable barriers

In a significant minority of cases the students described a physical barrier of some sort, usually a wall or a door which could not be breached, a physical affliction or an enemy of some kind.

It's a bit like a brick wall that just gets in the way all the time. It just stops you getting what you want.

It's like a maze with no entrance.

Sometimes this would become personalized.

It's like a bully pushing you around, not letting you do things . . . like the little gremlins from the (TV) reading advert where they say 'Reading – You don't like that!

In its most extreme form, a boy demonstrating quite severe signs of depression described his vision of dyslexia as

A head with a knife though it, split on two sides with a knife going through the middle. There's another head with a head inside – the one on the inside sad and the one on the outside happy.'

It can be seen that many of the metaphorical descriptions were accompanied by powerful, most often negative feelings, which we have termed *emotional reactions*. Again, these are sometimes straightforward, sometimes less so.

It's an annoying thing.

It's the word 'mafs' on fire.

Colourful but also with distress in it.

There are two heads – one sad, one happy.

A big book with Satan beside it. All the letters are gibberish.

Less emotionally laden responses most often reflected varying degrees of *cognitive confusion* and continuing lack of understanding.

It's a head with a muddled brain.

A colourful picture with a foggy veil over it.

Numbers with question marks.

A total mystery blob of paint.

A wooden, bendy chair – in a way, dyslexics bend.

Often, responses categorized under this heading were *personalized* or described as some form of individual or group reactions.

A person sitting at a table with a big question mark above their head with a maths book.

A confused looking person looking in a book.

It's someone having trouble, constantly putting their hand up.

People studying in a classroom. The people at the back, the dyslexics, need some help. The non-dyslexics sit at the front.

Here also the theme of *isolation* occasionally manifested itself.

I'd draw one person that's the odd one out.

It's like a person trying their hardest to do something and still the teacher saying that it isn't acceptable.

Just someone smart trying to do something they can't. They can't get out what they're trying to do.

This use of metaphor was surprisingly effective in bringing to life the students' feelings about dyslexia. At the same time it added a further qualitative dimension to the information that was being revealed from other sources about how well each individual had worked through their early confusion and was able to see dyslexia as a challenge that could somehow be met or was continuing to struggle with a sense of confusion and inevitable failure.

Initial and continuing responses of significant others

It is clear that the socio-cultural environment in which the dyslexic child grows up is vitally important in determining whether that child constructs a view of himself as a person of worth and capable of learning. It is here that the roots of self-efficacy or learned helplessness are set.

The most significant adults are undoubtedly the child's parents, most usually the mother, who have themselves to carry the burden of pushing hard for action on behalf of their offspring. The second important theme to emerge from the boys' narratives was what a vital role this came to be in providing support and encouragement in the face of apparent indifference, neglect and even hostility from elsewhere.

When we asked our dyslexic students to indicate the level of understanding about their difficulties that they felt each of their parents showed, we obtained the results shown in Table 4.1.

Table 4.1 Level of understanding shown by dyslexic students' parents

| | % responses | | | | |
	YES	yes	?	no	NO
My mother really understands how I feel	66	18	10	4	2
My father really understands how I feel	46	22	18	6	8

We can see from this that there is a high level of perceived support-ive understanding on the part of both sets of parents, but more strongly shown by mothers. The following quotes help to illustrate the appreciation that many boys felt for their parents' support.

Alex (13 years 3 months: Year 8)

My mum has helped me the most. I just talk to her a lot.

Simon (13 years 10 months: Year 9)

Most probably my mum has helped me most. She's very kind and always there for me, really. She got books and read about it. She found out about it and told me. She learned ways of dealing with it and just helped me.

By contrast, the statement 'The teachers at my last school really under-stood my difficulties' received a positive response from 14% of the boys and a strongly positive response from only 24%, in contrast to 26% who responded negatively and 26% who responded very nega-tively. Given that about 40% of the boys had transferred from specialist independent schools for dyslexic pupils, these findings give continu-ing cause for concern. The following quotes are fairly typical of many boys' responses.

Oliver (14 years 6 months: Year 9)

... one of my headteachers in my first school – I was in a state primary school – they didn't know I was dyslexic until I was about 10 when I went to a spe-cial school – and when they found out (I was dyslexic) the headteacher said there was no such thing as dyslexia, just stupid.

Andy (11 years 9 months: Year 7)

... the teacher used to bully me. Not the other kids. It did not get better. My mum said I would be tested, but he still did not take any notice.

The parents' perspectives

A study carried out by Griffiths, Norwich and Burden (2004) on behalf of the British Dyslexia Association (BDA), sponsored by the Buttle Trust, provides illumination on the perspectives of parents of dyslexic children in relation to those of teachers and local education authority representatives. A mismatch was often found between the concerns and expectations of the parents, which were focused on the needs of their own children, and the attitudes of the professionals, who tended to see the child as one of many and to judge his/her needs accordingly. In a disturbing number of cases, even in local education authorities with carefully planned policies in regard to all children with special educational needs, parental concerns were met with a feeling that they were overreacting or with the message that matters (i.e. the development of literacy) would take care of themselves in time. Growing parental concerns about their children's emotional reactions were often interpreted initially by professionals as being connected with factors other than the child's frustration with their learning difficulties, even to the extent of blaming the parents for the behavioural manifestations of the problems.

In such cases there was an inevitable breakdown in relationships and two-way loss of trust and understanding. What tended to follow is that parents began to develop their own strategies for securing appropriate educational provision for their children, which may well have led to their becoming more knowledgeable than many professionals about the nature, causes and even best educational practice in dealing with dyslexia. In this way the parents, most usually mothers, of dyslexic children develop unique aspects of their own sense of identity.

These findings support the results of a recent unpublished study by the present author in which the mothers of thirty children referred for independent psychological assessment for dyslexia described their own interactions with their children's teachers and schools. Almost all the mothers interviewed claim to have been convinced that there was something seriously wrong with their child's educational development before the child's eighth birthday, with only one having been informed by the school. The overwhelming memory of a further 70% of this sample was of lack of help or advice from professionals, with dawning awareness tending to come as a result of newspaper articles, television programmes, books or conversations with other parents.

Comments from these mothers such as 'The local school was most unhelpful', 'The school was not helpful saying she would grow out of it. There was a reluctance even when she was eight to have her assessed', were very much in line with those emerging from the BDA/Buttle Trust research.

Following formal diagnosis by an educational psychologist or specialist teacher, the predominant reaction amongst most parents was one of relief even though the response of teachers to a diagnosis was by no means always positive. Nevertheless, the great majority of mothers (80%) considered that the diagnosis of dyslexia had been helpful to their children for a variety of reasons ranging from greater understanding of the children's problems, increased confidence and extra help to access to appropriate schooling. Examples of comments made here were:

> It made our approach more positive.

> It gave L. confidence in herself and got her into a school that recognized dyslexia.

> I could help and understand and be more patient with B. – and advise teachers of the situation.

> Although the junior school did not accept the report, a more positive approach was adopted by the secondary school a few months later.

About 40% of the mothers in this survey felt that their children had responded well emotionally from the moment they had been diagnosed as dyslexic. Just under 20% considered that there had been early difficulties and some problems along the way, but only 10% reported continuing long-term difficulties. These problems appear to have been generated in large part by the negative attitudes of others and by inflexible requirements within the education system with regard to written assignments (especially where spelling was concerned), lack of support and lack of understanding.

Parental action

One of the most significant findings of the Buttle Trust research by Griffiths et al. (2004) was that even in local education authorities with strong dyslexia-friendly policies everything hinged upon the attitudes, knowledge and skill of individual teachers. Where primary school teachers were sensitive to the specific needs of all their pupils, there was often shared concern between those teachers and the dyslexic pupils' parents which would lead to appropriate action or intervention such as calling in an educational psychologist. Unfortunately, all too often the parents had had to battle with both schools and local authorities in order to have their concerns about their children's progress taken seriously, as the following examples show.

Daniel (15 years 5 months: Year 10)

My mum has always said that she thinks I had something wrong with my spelling and stuff, but my schools used to say there was nothing wrong with me and it was just behaviour and stuff. They wouldn't listen and she's been trying for eleven years, I think, to get me a statement. The comprehensive school was the worst. They didn't help me, they just gave me books and told me to get on with it. I've got books for the Tribunal with their comments saying 'You've got to put more effort in if you wanna stay in this class' and stuff. And a teacher sent me out of a class once for not understanding the work. She explained it and I asked her again. She said 'You weren't listening properly', so it made me feel mad.

Andy (11 years 9 months: Year 7)

The headmaster in my primary school did not want to know I was dyslexic. My mum first thought it was when I was about 8. I just wasn't interested in work. Mum arranged for a man to test me. After the tests he said I was dyslexic.

Interestingly, there were few examples of bullying or teasing by other children recalled by our sample. On the contrary, they often saw themselves as getting on perfectly well with their peers throughout their school careers and referred to non-dyslexic friends as being very understanding.

James (14 years: Year 10)

When I was a lot younger in Year 1 and 2 I got teased a tiny bit, but it was only a small school and as I got older my classmates kind of got used to it.

Simon (13 years 10 months: Year 9)

I never got teased by the other kids. It didn't bother me at first because I didn't know much about dyslexia then. I just thought, 'Oh, ok.'... I didn't get told I was dyslexic till I moved out of my old school. When I found out, I rang up all my friends and told them I was dyslexic and they were all fine about it. They just said 'Oh'.

Joe (14 years 3 months: Year 10)

> I wasn't teased (at my old school) 'cos I had my own gang, but I made a
> menace of myself. The girls used to tease me more than the boys 'cos I'd
> never hit a girl.

The effects of such interactions clearly paid a further significant part in
the dyslexic boys' level of adjustment to their difficulties and their
developing sense of identity.

Subsequent action

At this point in their learning careers the introduction of a specialist
teacher and/or educational psychologist most commonly takes place.
If it does not, then further frustration inevitably occurs and despair
may even set in.

John (14 years 3 months: Year 10)

> I was getting into loads of trouble. I was beating up kids. I was having to go
> out of lessons to get help and all that sort of stuff. My mum knew she was
> dyslexic, but because there was so much bad press about it at the time, she
> ignored it and pretended she wasn't. Then she looked into the matter and
> had me looked at and got herself looked at, at the same time to see how
> severely dyslexic we were. I got seen by a psychologist but we had to fight
> for three years against the local authority to get something done. Then we
> won (a tribunal case) and got to this school and things went really well.

Alan (12 years 10 months: Year 8)

> When I was diagnosed they said my brain was like a path I had to go along
> but there was a bull walking in the way, so I had to find other ways round.
> It sort of made sense. Everyone used to say I was stupid, but when I found
> out I was dyslexic, no-one could say that any more.

Change of school

The next step is likely to be a transfer of schooling, either, if the parents can afford it, to a specialist school for dyslexics at the primary
stage or to secondary school. As the current philosophical emphasis in
education is on social and educational inclusion for all, it is highly
unlikely that local authorities will be willing to support financially

transfer to a specialist secondary school for dyslexics in the first instance. However, if the child's level of disability is manifestly great and the specialist teaching on offer limited or non-existent, some financial backing may occasionally be forthcoming. What is far more likely, however, is that the parents will once again be rebuffed and forced to make considerable financial sacrifices to obtain appropriate specialist education for their children if they consider it necessary.

An important further consideration arises here. Special schools for dyslexics tend to be small, independent, residential and necessarily very expensive due to the perceived need for small classes and intensive one-to-one input by highly qualified teachers. Under such circumstances, there is a need to provide evidence of value for money, i.e. successful educational outcomes of some kind.

The nature of those hoped-for outcomes is somewhat more complex than might appear at first sight. An improved standard of literacy and/or numeracy without a doubt. But what standard of improvement can reasonably be expected of a boy (or girl), however intelligent, who at the age of 11 can barely read, spell or write coherently, or who struggles to make sense of even the most basic mathematical transactions? What might be the chances of achieving good results across a range of subjects in GCSE examinations at the age of 16? Is it enough, moreover, just to provide intensive remedial input of multi-sensory teaching with information and computer technology (ICT) back-up, or is something else needed to help the students become more positive in their attitudes towards school subjects at which they had continually failed for at least six years and more confident in their own chances of success? What can psychological theories tell us about how this might best be accomplished and measured? These issues are ones that were addressed in the second phase of the research project on which this book is based, which will be described in the next chapter.

A first step towards answering some of these questions relates to what some psychologists consider to be one of the most important aspects of motivation – the element of *choice* (Ames, 1992). How much opportunity did the boys in our sample have to choose to attend this particular school and did they continued to feel satisfied with their choice?

David (14 years 6 months: Year 10)

At my last school I was having a lot of difficulty with writing and spelling and things like that, so we looked around for a school that would help me with it and we found (this one) and I started to come here . . . it's smaller, you get more time with the teacher, the hours are longer here, I don't have to go home and do my homework but I do it here and they know more about your individual difficulties so they can focus on them and help you in different ways.

Greg (14 years: Year 9)

... it's just really good, it's just like a normal school and you get really special help an' everything . . . so you don't have to . . . like . . . all previous schools you had to, like, be taken out of school to, like, Dyslexia Institutes and stuff like that, and here you don't, you just feel normal like everyone's in the same position. I like that.

Keith (12 years 8 months: Year 7)

I liked that people listened to you and understand how you feel and everyone was the same. We looked at a usual comprehensive school but I didn't want to go there 'cos I'd be different and have to go out of class for extra help.

Tom (13 years: Year 8)

I came to see this school myself and thought it was really good 'cos the classes were so small and, like, you knew everybody's name and everybody was very kind.

Sam (13 years 10 months: Year 9)

I started in the local primary school but didn't settle so I moved to a private school in Year 6. In Year 8 I just started messing about and I didn't concentrate. Then I had a test that found out I was dyslexic, so I got asked to leave to go to a dyslexic school. So I looked around and found this one on the Internet . . . All the other schools' websites were pretty basic (but this one) was very interesting. The website told you a lot about dyslexia and explained a lot and it showed you all around the school and it was interactive. So I decided to pay a visit and came here for a day and liked it, so I came . . . This school was just different. It was more relaxed, more calm and just completely different from my old school.

Positive comments were also made about the specialist nature of the school in contrast to mainstream education.

William (14 years: Year 10)

It's a lot easier to get on top of it (in a school like this) because you haven't got the pressure of having a separate thing, something that no one else has.

(In my last school) I was the only one in the house that had that – I was in a special set called the 'F' set, which didn't help because it was known as the bottom set and you were branded as being stupid because you were in that set.

Alex (13 years 3 months: Year 8)

It's all boys here (and) everyone understands how you feel. You've all been through, like, the same stuff, so you all know what it feels like, so you can all talk together without anyone taking the mick or anything. They say that you work better when it's all the same sex and it does work.

Support for this positive nature of these statements is provided by the nature of the boys' responses to the statement 'The teachers at this school really understand my difficulties'. Here 86% showed strong agreement, 10% mild agreement, with none disagreeing at all.

Reaching adolescence

By this point in their learning careers dyslexics will almost certainly have established a core set of self-constructs about themselves as learners which will be related to the sense they make of their successes and failures (their attributions), their confidence in their ability to be successful at tasks at which they may have previously failed (self-efficacy versus learned helplessness), their degree of optimism about their future prospects (lack of depression), their sense of being in control of their own destiny (locus of control), the amount of effort they are prepared to put in to achieve a desired educational outcome (motivation) and their awareness of appropriate strategies to employ to achieve those outcomes (metacognition). All of these factors together can be seen as contributing to the dyslexic person's academic self-concept and self-esteem. We will now turn to the results of the assessment of these factors in our special school population.

CHAPTER 5

How it feels to be dyslexic

We now have a set of techniques to make possible the assessment of dyslexic individuals' sense of identity. We also have as our first sample population a significant number of adolescent boys with confirmed dyslexic difficulties attending a small specialist independent school. Further information which subsequently came to light was that the school has built a remarkable reputation for achieving well above average success rates in GCSE public examinations prior to the boys moving on at the age of 16. Our population, therefore, consists of a mixed group of academic failures (on entry to the school) and potential successes (prior to sitting examinations). The number of boys interviewed in each year is shown in Table 5.1.

Table 5.1 Number of boys interviewed in each year group

Year group	Age range	Number
7	11–12	8
8	12–13	8
9	13–14	13
10	14–15	14
11	15–16	7

Before providing a breakdown of the boys' response to the various questionnaires, it might prove helpful to speculate on some possible outcomes. As has been revealed in Chapter 1, almost all the previous research studies in this area have found their dyslexic populations to have poor self-concepts, to be lacking in a sense of self-efficacy, to tend towards feelings of learned helplessness, to see the results of their efforts as being outside their control and to have a tendency towards a depressive outlook on life. However, here we have a school with a proven record of academic success. What relationship might we expect, therefore, between the students' academic self-concepts and sense of agency and their future success? Theoretically, it seems reasonable to hypothesize that the boys' academic self-concepts are most likely to be lower than average on entry to the school, but should begin to rise as they see the positive results of their efforts. At the same time, feelings of learned helplessness should decrease whilst feelings of self-efficacy and internal locus of control rise.

The results obtained from each section of the investigation will now be presented in turn before drawing them together to demonstrate the ways in which the different aspects of the boys' learning identities interacted.

Myself-as-a-Learner Scale (MALS)

The scale was completed by 46 boys; 10 in Year 8, 14 in Year 9 and 22 in Year 10.

Within the general secondary school population the average expected MALS score is in the region of 71 with a standard deviation of 10.5, i.e. an average score would lie between 60 and 82 (Burden, 1998).

In this sample the overall average score obtained was 62 with a standard deviation of 12.3, i.e. the average score lay between 50 and 74. This suggests that even in a first-class special school with considerable individual help the academic self-concept of adolescent boys with learning difficulties of a dyslexic nature is likely to be in the region of 10 points or one standard deviation lower than would normally be found in the general population. However, if we break these scores down into averages for each year group, a somewhat different picture begins to emerge, as is shown in Table 5.2.

Table 5.2 Average MALS scores for each year group

Year 8 mean score ($n = 10$)	57.9 SD 14.6
Year 9 mean score ($n = 14$)	66.5 SD 11.1
Year 10 mean score ($n = 22$)	68.5 SD 11.8

What this appears to suggest is that as most boys enter the school in Year 8, their academic self-concept starts to strengthen and grow the longer they remain at the school. Some degree of confirmatory evidence is provided by the fact that within Year 8 seven boys obtained MALS scores significantly below the average score of the standardization sample, whilst in Year 9 only three boys obtained such low scores, and in Year 10 four.

We cannot assume too much from these data, however, as the results are cross-sectional, not longitudinal. It may be, for example, that this particular Year 8 group differ in certain important ways from the boys in Years 9 and 10. Only by following them through over several years could we tell whether there was an actual improvement in self-concept. What these figures do suggest, however, is that the academic self-concept does not necessarily remain constant, but is likely to shift in a positive or negative direction in line with (lack of) developing skills, (lack of) increased attainment and (lack of) growth of self-confidence and learner autonomy. It also suggests that learner self-concept is likely to be, at least to a certain extent, context specific, i.e. quite strongly mediated by factors existing within the home, school and classroom environment.

At the moment these results can be considered no more than speculative, but they do raise worthwhile avenues for further research. One step taken in this direction was to administer the MALS to 37 students with recorded specific learning difficulties (a term preferred by the local education authority) attending two mainstream comprehensive schools in a nearby locality. Here a mean score of 60.8 with a standard deviation of 10.3 was recorded, which is slightly lower than that of our special school sample. Further research in this area is currently being carried out.

Self-efficacy/Locus of control

The strength of each individual's feelings about their competence and confidence to tackle the learning problems with which they were faced is measured by six items, according to a five-point scale ranging from 'strongly agree' to 'strongly disagree'. Table 5.3 shows the range of responses to each item on this subscale.

Here we can see that the vast majority of the boys interviewed were strongly disposed towards *effort* as an essential attribution for success, and that they demonstrate very strong *internal locus of control* with regard to success in examinations and their longer-term future. There are also clear indications of a growing confidence in their ability to

Table 5.3 Self-efficacy/locus of control (*n* = 50)

Item	% response				
	YES	yes	?	no	NO
If I try hard I can achieve as much as anyone else	76	18	6	0	0
I can be good at maths if I really want to	60	20	4	14	2
I can be good at English if I really want to	30	50	10	6	4
I have the ability to do well in exams if I want to	68	24	8	0	0
How well I do in the future is up to me	88	12	0	0	0
I know how I can overcome my learning difficulties	30	46	16	6	2

overcome their learning difficulties. Of some significance is the fact that they were rather more confident of their ability to do well in mathematics than in English, but again the indicators here were of a much more positive nature than would normally be expected.

Given that there are five response choices for each of the six items on this subscale, we can reasonably assume that a score increasingly above 18 is indicative of positive feelings of self-efficacy and internal locus of control, with scores of above 24 indicating particularly strong feelings of this nature. A score of 12 or less, on the other hand, can be safely considered as indicative of low self-efficacy and external locus of control.

When the scores of each year group were averaged out the following results shown in Table 5.4 were obtained.

Table 5.4 Average self-efficacy scores for each year group

Year group	Number	Mean score
7	8	25.8
8	8	26.1
9	13	25.0
10	14	25.9
11	7	26.7

No significant differences were found between any of these scores, all of which are indicative of very positive feelings of self-efficacy within each year group. Closer analysis revealed only two boys, one in Year 8 and one in Year 10, with borderline low scores. The case histories of these boys will be examined in more detail in the following chapter.

Learned helplessness

Feelings of learned helplessness are measured by means of three items, responses to which are shown in Table 5.5.

Table 5.5 Feelings of learned helplessness ($n = 50$)

Item	YES	% response			
		yes	?	no	NO
My dyslexia makes it impossible for me to do really well at school	0	6	4	20	70
However hard I try, I'll never be as good at schoolwork as someone who isn't dyslexic	12	16	20	20	32
I will always be held back by my dyslexic difficulties	4	24	16	18	38

These results suggest that learned helplessness does not appear to be a condition into which most of these students have fallen. The vast majority disagree with the implication that dyslexia poses for them an insurmountable barrier to doing well at school. However, there are indications that just over a quarter of the sample displayed lowered expectations about just how much they would be able to achieve in view of their dyslexia difficulties. Thus, their optimism is tinged with a realistic concern that the future will not be all plain sailing.

Given that there are five response choices for each of the three items on this subscale, we can reasonably assume that a score of above 9 is indicative of significant feelings of learned helplessness, whilst a score of 6 or less indicates that few such feelings are likely to exist. There is a fine line to be drawn here between realistic awareness of current and future obstacles which need to be overcome and a sense of growing despair that they seem to be insurmountable.

When the scores of each year group were averaged out, the results shown in Table 5.6 were obtained.

Table 5.6 Average learned helplessness scores of each year group

Year group	Number	Mean score
7	8	6.6
8	8	8.0
9	13	5.8
10	14	6.0
11	7	6.0

Despite the apparent indication of a greater sense of learned help-lessness amongst the Year 8 group, the differences between the average scores were not found to be statistically significant, which most probably reflects the small number of items on this subscale and the limited number of students responding in each age group. However, an examination of the individual scores revealed that four boys scored above 9 in Year 8, one in Years 7 and 10, and none in Years 9 and 11. This indicates that feelings of learned helplessness are apparent in about 12% of this population, a much lower incidence than previous research findings would lead us to expect. This is an important finding because it may indicate that the negative feelings of a small minority of dyslexic students may well have affected interpre-tations of previous research findings, especially if these were solely based on measures of central tendency producing average scores for the sample studied.

Depression

Feelings of depression may be revealed in a number of different ways and at several different levels. Table 5.7 shows the pattern of responses to each of the six items on the depression subscale.

Table 5.7 Indications of depressive tendencies ($n = 50$)

	% response				
Item	YES	yes	?	no	NO
I wish I wasn't dyslexic	22	12	28	16	22
Being dyslexic really bothers me	10	14	8	32	36
Before I came to this school I used to feel depressed about being dyslexic	16	12	10	18	44
Dyslexia is a curse	6	6	10	16	62
I keep wishing my dyslexia would go away	12	18	22	24	24
A lot of the time I feel depressed about being dyslexic	6	8	2	26	58

Here we can see that the boys were almost equally divided between those who wished that they were not dyslexic and those for whom it did not appear to invoke strong negative feelings. More than two-thirds denied that they were really bothered about their dyslexia and under a third admitted to wishing that it would go away. A small number felt strongly that dyslexia was a curse and made them feel depressed. The case histories of these boys will be examined in greater detail in the next chapter. Of particular note here is the fact that the feelings of depression had been halved since entry to the present school.

Given that there are five response choices for the six items on this subscale, we can reasonably assume that a score of above 18 is indicative of strong negative feelings about how it feels to be dyslexic, whilst scores of above 24 are likely to be pointers to feelings of deep depression. A score of 12 or less, on the other hand, can be taken as indicative of a more positive state of mind.

When the scores of each year group were averaged out, the results shown in Table 5.8 were obtained.

Table 5.8 Average depression scores of each year group

Year group	Number	Mean score
7	8	13.6
8	8	17.9
9	13	12.9
10	14	12.9
11	7	13.4

Again we can see that whilst most year groups demonstrate generally positive feelings about themselves, the Year 8 cohort display a greater degree of negativity. Closer analysis of the individual cases revealed one boy in Year 7 with a high depression index, three in Year 8, one in Year 9, one in Year 10 and none in Year 11, i.e. 12%, somewhat higher than the expected level in the general population. The individual case histories of these boys will be considered in greater detail in the next chapter.

Summary

What can we justifiably conclude from these results, given the limitations of the sampling procedure? What we have here is an opportunity sample of dyslexic boys attending a selective residential special school at great cost to their parents and, in a small number of cases, local education authorities. They are therefore almost certainly from a middle class background and the offspring of supportive parents who are prepared to find by whatever means the funding for their education. All the indications are that those parents and most of the boys themselves also chose very carefully what they felt would be the most appropriate school to meet the boys' needs. This can hardly, therefore, be considered a representative sample of dyslexic adolescents within the general population.

However, given that the thoughts and feelings of more than 60% of this school's population were surveyed, we can reasonably assume that we have strong evidence of how it can feel to be dyslexic under certain positive circumstances. In summary, therefore, we can state with confidence that in this school:

- the general level of academic self-concept is lower than would be normally expected in the secondary school population at large, but
- this self-concept is likely to increase significantly the longer the boys stay at the school;
- there is a clear sense of internal locus of control amongst the boys over their future academic success,
- a strong orientation towards effort as one of the chief contributions to success at schoolwork and examinations, and
- a belief in their own ability to achieve this success if this is the goal that they set for themselves;
- there are very few indications of feelings of learned helplessness
- or of more generalized depression relating to their dyslexic condition,
- although in one year group – Year 8, the year in which most boys join the school – there does appear to be a significant subgroup of boys who are vulnerable in each of these areas;
- the majority of boys felt that their difficulties were not properly understood by teachers at their previous school, and that
- most people did not understand how it felt to be dyslexic; however, almost all felt that their difficulties were really understood by the teachers at their present school;
- a sense of identity with other dyslexics is indicated by the feeling that only another dyslexic can understand how it feels to be dyslexic; finally

- the vast majority of boys identify their mothers as understanding how they feel, with slightly less but still the majority, feeling understood by their fathers.

The significance of these findings and their educational implications will be considered in the final chapter.

CHAPTER 6

Boys' own stories

In this chapter we present the personal narratives of five boys in order to illustrate both the uniqueness of their stories and the similar threads running through them. We do this to emphasize the point that however confident we may become in describing the commonalities in the experiences of dyslexics during their education careers and in predicting the most likely outcomes of this, we can but should never overlook the fact that every life history is unique in its own particular way. These particular stories have been selected because they each reveal the strength of taking a triangulated approach to gathering data whereby questionnaire results and more qualitative data of an open-ended nature can complement each other in revealing a more rounded picture of the individual student.

David's story

David is a slightly built, friendly, but somewhat inarticulate 15-year-old who gives the impression of having some expressive language difficulties. His father has retired and his mother works in a professional capacity which involves a great deal of travelling. He has two sisters and a brother and believes that both his elder brother and his father may be dyslexic. His MALS score is within the average range (65) and he shows no signs of depression or strong feelings of learned helplessness, but he does display a lack of confidence in his ability to do well in his schoolwork and a tendency towards an external locus of control. Significantly, within the MALS he conveyed that he did not like having problems to solve and was not very good at it. He also found learning difficult and did not feel confident in working out what to do when he got stuck. By contrast, he was proud of his sporting prowess at rugby and, particularly, cross-country running. He has been at the present school for two years.

The sentence completion items provided a number of positive indicators, e.g. 'The best thing that has happened to me . . . *is coming to this school.*' 'When I leave school . . . *I want to be successful.*' 'How would you change in any way? *I wouldn't.*' He indicated clearly, moreover, that he much preferred practical subjects and sport to maths and English. His main attributions for doing well at school were 'the teachers at this school and my confidence because I came here'. His reasons for not doing well were 'I maybe haven't been working enough on it (the work) or maybe I haven't been concentrating in my head.' David's personal account of his learning career took the following form:

> My mum has always said that she thinks I had something wrong with my spelling and stuff, but my schools used to say there was nothing wrong with me and it was just behaviour and stuff. They wouldn't listen and she'd been trying for eleven years, I think, to get me a statement. We moved to the South-West because it was nearer to my mum's work.
>
> Dyslexia means the ability, the disability to write, read and understand as well as a normal age group. But most people dyslexic are higher IQ than a normal person. I've got 'A' in Year 8 . . . when I first got assessed about my dyslexia they did a load of tests. A special person told me the results. A lot of dyslexics, they know the answers and stuff but they can't get it out. I can't write as normal people, neat and I can't write consistent, like all the same, and I can't read big words very well, but I have got a good knowledge of words. (My picture of dyslexia is) just someone smart trying to do something they can't. They can't get what they're trying to do . . . All I imagine is just someone sat there who's smart but can't do it. It's not really an object or anything.
>
> I didn't understand what it was at first, not completely, but I got to know it a bit more. I knew it was a learning disability. My mum had helped me understand it most and this school has helped me a lot. (After I was diagnosed) I felt a bit relieved 'cos I knew what was wrong and I knew what to work on. The previous school still said I wasn't dyslexic even though I'd been tested by some of the best doctors in the country. I've forgotten his name, but I went to his house and it cost a lot of money, like £500. He's one of the best in the country. Even when he said I was dyslexic, they still said no.
>
> The comprehensive were the worst. They didn't help me, they just gave me books and told me to get on with it. I've got books for the Tribunal with their comments saying 'You've got to put more effort in if you wanna stay in this class' and stuff. And a teacher sent me out and I asked her again. She said 'You weren't listening properly' so it made me feel mad. It was a bit annoying when I got asked to read out loud. It was embarrassing.

I moved from that college at the end of Year 8 to here. My mum wanted to get some proper help and stuff for me so she looked at all the schools for dyslexia and stuff and she found this was the best so she sent me to this one. I came to the school for a day. It was a lot smaller than what I was used to (nearly 2000 students). (There was) good stuff to look at outside instead of just fences and that. The boarding was a bit dodgy at first. It took a couple of months (to settle). I used to get really homesick but now I'm not bothered at all. I've got used to it now. I'm definitely glad I came. I've done loads. The people (make it special). They teach you really well and they understand you and help you with all your work. Special school is good 'cos you're around all the same learning abilities, aren't you? There's no need to get embarrassed or anything. It's just a lot easier and you don't have to worry about standing up and reading.

(Whether dyslexia can be cured) depends what sort of dyslexic you are and what areas. How the person feels. I feel it can be to a certain point, but you can't be normal like, like a normal person. You can't go straight there, but you can get near to it. You can't just take a pill or something like that . . . It's like a little kid growing up – that sort of thing.

(To get better) you must try to do what the teachers tell you. Like, in this school it's a lot different to what the other teachers said, so I just try. They'll help you and tell you ways how to break it down a lot easier, like covering it up, like all this stuff.

I do tell other people I'm dyslexic. They sometimes ask a few questions. If you (just) say I can't read or write, they think you're stupid, you can only do ABC and all that, but dyslexic means I'm smarter than them.

There are good things about being dyslexic. You get the opportunity to be heard more if you go to the right place. Einstein was dyslexic. A lot of people who lacks confidence. So, it is good in a way if you come to a place where people understand you and you'll get a better education than normal people, I think.

Lots of dyslexics (are gifted in other ways). For me it's sport. I'm a good runner and a good sports player. A lot of people here are really good at something. It's sport or computer games or something.

(In the future) I want to do something practical instead of sitting in an office, like. I was thinking of being an architect, but it would be too much sitting around. My brother's going in the RAF, so I might take up that. I'd be good in that.

Michael's story

Michael is an articulate 12-year-old, thoughtful and quite big for his age. His father is an engineer. Two elder brothers have a history of learning difficulties. He is in his second term at the school, where he arrived late due to difficulties in obtaining funding which were eventually resolved following a tribunal hearing. His academic self-concept score on the MALS is low (52) and reveals a generally poor perception of his general learning ability. Fairly strong positive responses were recorded to most self-efficacy items but Michael was less confident in his ability to be good at maths or in knowing how to overcome his learning difficulties. This was borne out by an unusually high learned helplessness score (13), where he indicated that he felt he would never be as good at school work as someone who was not dyslexic, however hard he tried, and that his dyslexia made it impossible to do really well at school. An extremely high score was also obtained on the depression subscale (28), which would not necessarily have been picked up from his fairly bland responses to more open-ended questioning.

> I can't remember how it was first found out I was dyslexic. I think my teacher mentioned it to my parents 'cos she had a dyslexic son, and . . . she mentioned it to some people and they put me forward to a psychologist test which confirmed I was dyslexic.
>
> It was very difficult because we were in a class of 30 odd people and you would sit there and try and do the work but you just couldn't, and the teacher didn't have the time to help you, and they got a dictaphone to help me and I used to sit in the teacher's cupboard and do my stories into the dictaphone. It's all very well, that's good, but it wasn't improving my English at all. To improve something you have to do more of it and you can't help your writing by talking, can you? The other kids were OK with me. They didn't use to tease me. I've got two brothers, 18 and 17, and the older one went through the whole of school without his dyslexia being noticed. The other one is dyspraxic and you can't read his handwriting at all. I find writing really hard (but) I've got a lot better at reading. I used to be really shy, but going to the special school has helped me. I've got really bad spelling too.
>
> I can't honestly remember how I felt (when I was diagnosed). Being called dyslexic doesn't really make me feel any different. I understand now what it means. It's a learning difficulty that some people have, and you get lots of different types of dyslexia. Some people find it hard to remember things and maybe it takes you longer to learn to read and it's harder for you to like, write and it takes longer for everything to come into your mind. You see things in a different way sometimes to what other people would. It's like quite a lot of dyslexic people are good with computers because you see things in a different way so you can make it in a different way. I really enjoy making things. I don't know yet what I want to do (in the future), but I want to be out doing something, not kind of sat not doing anything, sat at a desk typing into a computer.

After I got a statement I went to a place called the B . . . Dyslexia Centre. I used to go for, like, 3 hour lessons a week. Then we found out there was a school there and I went to the school full time after that. Two people that are here used to go to my old school and my parents found out about it. I came for a day about a year ago and I liked it, but we had to go through all the tribunal and stuff to get me here, so I'm paid for now, but that's why I came late. We had to go through a long battle to get here. By changing schools things got better because I had the specialist help and I was around people that totally understand what it was, because you can't help somebody that's dyslexic if you don't know about dyslexia, basically.

This school is designed purposely for dyslexic people so you get the help you need and they understand your problems. When I came to see it, everyone was friendly and the teachers all understood you properly and they showed you they could help you with what needs you have and everything. I'm glad I came. I know that some people that are dyslexic have to go to a school with 30 people in a class and they just sit there and don't learn anything. But here you're only in a class of a few people and if you don't understand something you can just put your hand up and they'll explain it for you and stuff like that.

I don't think you can cure dyslexia, but you can help it – by special schooling like this and by having self-confidence. If you think you can beat it, you will, but you can never get rid of it. It will always be there. I think of it like an onion. It's got lots of different layers. One layer may be good and one layer may be, like, half there, and one might not be. And, say, if you put a layer on, it would, like, peel off, kind of thing. And you'd have to stick it back on with, like, Pritt Stick, and, like, hold it there a while to make sure it stays.

Wesley's story

Wesley is in his second year at the present school (Year 8). He is over-weight and displays many signs of being quite severely depressed, as the following interview shows. However, there would appear to be several indications that this depression is not totally attributable to his dyslexic condition.

Wesley's mother is French, his father is English. They are now separated. His father pays the school fees, but his mother has been particularly helpful and supportive. She was a translator, but is now a hospital counsellor, and is fluent in several languages.

Wesley considers that he reads French better than English. He believes that one of his uncles is dyslexic. Both he and his brother have been diagnosed as dyspraxic.

Wesley scored particularly poorly on the MALS (score: 44), well below the mainstream average and even significantly low compared with his dyslexic peers. On the positive side he saw himself as quite good at discussing things and at learning the meanings of lots of words, and quite liked using his brain. The vast majority of his responses were negative (7) or very negative (6), where he indicated a complete lack of confidence in his ability to do new work or to solve the problems that he met. Learning was considered to be very difficult. He did indicate also, however, that he was clever in some ways.

On the self-efficacy/locus of control scale, Wesley scored at just above the borderline level but did indicate that he saw his future as being in his own hands. He again showed his ambivalence on the learned helplessness items, but clearly felt that he would always be held back by his dyslexic difficulties. It was on the items relating to feelings of depression, however, that the depth of Wesley's misery became apparent, with an extreme negative score being recorded against each item. All of these items relate to the negative consequences of dyslexia, but Wesley also revealed in his responses to sentence completion items that his weight was a big issue for him as it had led to his being teased and bullied for being fat. There were, nevertheless, some positive signs. He saw the best thing that had happened to him had been 'coming to this school and getting the lead role in a play'. He was also enjoying drama, art and music, in sharp contrast to maths and English. His own personal narrative built upon many of these issues.

When I was at primary school I used to get bullied for being fat. I was unhappy so I ate a lot. When I was in France a doctor found I was asthmatic, but the GP in England refused to accept the diagnosis. Then I had a big asthma attack. I've tried to get my weight down with exercise and diets but nothing works. I hate myself as I am.

When I was about seven my mum suspected I was dyslexic, so I went to see a lady in her office who assessed me. I don't know if she was a psychologist or a teacher. I used to be bullied before that. I was called stupid. I still got bullied about my weight.

After I was diagnosed we looked for a dyslexic school. We found one in London with smaller classes. It was good at the primary level but didn't have secondary specialist teachers, so we had to look around again. We found this one and liked the atmosphere on the boarding side. This is the first time I've been a boarder.

My mum explained about dyslexia to me right from the beginning so I understood it. She has helped me most to understand it. It's a problem with reading, writing and spelling. (The picture in my mind is) a head with a knife through it. It's split into two on two sides with the knife going through the middle. There's another head with the head inside. The one on the inside is sad and the one on the outside is happy.

The best thing about this school is that the teachers understand about dyslexic needs and explain things properly and don't get angry. When the school and teachers don't know that you're dyslexic they put you in the bottom groups where the work is really easy and uninteresting – in a specialist school they give you difficult work but explain it properly. You can't cure dyslexia but you can get better if you work hard and get the right teaching.

(In the future) I want to be an embalmer. It pays well and no-one wants to do the job. I read a book about an embalmer once, who struggled with no friends because of the type of job, but that wouldn't bother me.

Edwin's story

Edwin's father is in the Forces, currently based overseas. He has one younger brother. He thinks that his father and his brother are slightly dyslexic. He gave the impression initially of being rather anxious, but tried to indicate that everything was fine for him.

Contradictions appeared in his responses to different aspects of the interview, as will be apparent. His is currently in Year 8 and has been at the present school for a year.

I started school at the village school but transferred to (A) school for dyslexics in Year 6. I can't remember why. My mum organized it. One of the teachers in my first school gave me extra help. I took some tests but I can't remember anything about them. I've done lots of tests since then. The Army pays the fees.

I transferred from (A) when my family moved to abroad. My mum and dad came to look at (this) school and arranged for me to spend a bit of time here – a day and a night. I liked it. I knew lots of people who had come here from my last school. There's more freedom than at (A). You can go down to the village, have TVs in your room, do more stuff. I'm glad I came.

Dyslexia means learning difficulties with English and maths. My difficulties are mainly with spelling. (I see) dyslexia (as) an annoying thing . . . because I have to travel a long way to go to school. I think it can be cured, given time. You can make it better, but it will still be there. You get over it by sheer hard work and determination.

I've never been upset about it. I just don't feel anything. I never had a problem with my early teachers. My parents have helped me most to understand it – and my brother. We get on well. He's also at a boarding school but isn't so dyslexic as me.

I don't say much about it really to other people 'cos I can't explain it particularly well. It's just difficulty in learning.

Am I especially good at other things? Yeah, I'm particularly good at shooting. My dad's a member of the British Shooting Association. I went to one of their days when you can try out different things. The shooting instructor suggested I should get lessons.

The future? I haven't a clue.

This fairly bland, reasonably upbeat account is contradicted by Edwin's responses to more direct questioning. In responses to sentence completion items, for example, he stated 'I'm really happy when I'm at home. I'm miserable when I'm at school. The best thing that has happened to me is . . . going home. If I could change myself in any way . . . I'd get rid of my dyslexia.'

His MALS score was extremely low (score: 37), well below even the average special school level. The one positive response was to the statement 'I'm good at discussing things.' There was some ambivalence about feeling clever and feeling confident about tackling new work, but all other items were answered at the extreme negative level.

Somewhat surprisingly, Edwin scored well on the self-efficacy scale, but this was contradicted by a borderline learned helplessness score, where he indicated that he felt he would always be held back by his dyslexic difficulties and never be as good at schoolwork as someone who was not dyslexic. There were, moreover, a number of strong indications of depressive feelings of an ongoing nature.

Overall, this is a picture of a lad who is struggling to put a brave face on the fact that he misses family life and even the companionship of his brother, which he mainly blames on his dyslexic condition. Beneath it all, however, is a very low academic self-concept and a general tendency towards feeling depressed.

Noel's story

Noel is Irish, a member of a large extended family with relatives in Scotland and the West of England. He has an older brother who he thinks is slightly dyslexic and a sister who does not appear to be. His grandfather is dyslexic also but is a self-made successful businessman who provides the fees for all of his seven grandchildren to attend private schools.

Noel is 13 years old and currently in Year 8 of his present school, which he only joined this year. It would appear that his learning difficulties were picked up by a remedial teacher at an early age (about 6), but for the next five years or so he learnt very little.

We looked for a school in Ireland but couldn't find anything there to help dyslexics. There is one school but it's not very good, so we looked for a school in Scotland (where granddad lives). We tried a school in Newcastle for a term but it wasn't very convenient.

A friend of mum's a psychologist. He assessed me and recommended this school. I'm glad I came. The teaching is better than the Scotland school. You're not the lowest in the class. In my old school they'd give some work then leave you for five minutes and then move on to something else when you've not finished. Because this is a dyslexic school you fit in much better, so that's good.

(Dyslexia means) people who don't pick up work so easy – not all work, just reading or writing or spelling. Maths is hard too. I get extra help for maths in and out of class.

Noel's MALS score is low (48), but this is mainly made up of 'yes and no' responses linked with strongly negative responses to items relating to finding work difficult, needing lots of help and not seeing himself as at all clever. He did claim, however, to enjoy using his brain and liking having problems to solve. He scored positively on self-efficacy and locus of control items and showed few signs of depressive tendencies, but there were indications of learned helplessness in that he strongly agreed with the statements 'However hard I try, I'll never be as good at school work as someone who isn't dyslexic' and 'I will always be held back by my dyslexic difficulties.'

Noel's metaphor for dyslexia was fairly prosaic:

I think it would be like a kid that doesn't understand his work. Like people who are trying extra hard because they don't understand. Not like normal people who are not dyslexic.

I can't remember much about my primary school. No-one really helped me understand (my dyslexia), I just picked it up by myself. The other kids have always been fine. My friends understand, they know what it is. You can't cure it but you can get better by trying hard and not letting it bother you. When I do well at my work it's because I try very hard, like in rugby. When I don't do well it's through not trying hard in lessons or not trying to win at games or not listening to the teacher.

(When I leave school) I want to join the army as an engineer to serve the country. They give you free training to become an engineer and I could get a scholarship. You get quite a lot of money for being in the army.

CHAPTER 7
Pulling it all together

This book was started with a number of related aims. Its first intention was to highlight the importance of people's self-concept in their lives in shaping their sense of identity, whilst at the same time revealing some of the major difficulties involved in defining what is meant by the terms 'self-concept' and 'self-esteem' and in attempts to measure them. In this endeavour I have drawn upon a number of theoretical perspectives from the social sciences, in particular socio-cultural theory, symbolic interactionism and research and theory in the areas of motivation and attitudes.

In reviewing just a very small proportion of the hundreds of articles providing evidence of the association between aspects of self-concept and educational achievement I also provide an overview of the much less extensive literature demonstrating the negative connection between self-concept and dyslexia or learning disability. Although we are not in a position as yet to be able to invoke a causative relationship between the two, the bulk of previous research evidence clearly demonstrates that dyslexics are likely to suffer from comparatively poor academic self-concepts, a weak sense of self-efficacy, feelings of learned helplessness and even a tendency towards depression. What is clear from much of this research, however, is that the findings tend to be based upon measures of central tendency in which the average scores of dyslexic groups compare unfavourably with those of control or comparison groups who are not manifesting dyslexic symptoms or learning difficulties. Assumptions are often then made, sometimes without justification, about the emotional reactions of dyslexics in general and/or about simplistic cause and effect relationships. There have also been quite evident problems in identifying appropriate techniques for assessing the self-perceptions and psychological well-being of dyslexics and others with learning difficulties of whatever nature.

The need for a different approach to research in this area has been well summarized by Herrington and Hunter-Carsch (2001, p. 115) in the following way:

> We would prefer a research/assessment/teaching framework in which the multi-faceted, dynamic nature of dyslexia is recognised and explored ...
>
> • including more than literacy difficulties;
> • involving more than the characteristic cognitive profile;
> • including whole-person factors and the developing dynamics of the cognitive-affective constellation with 'personality' aspects;
> • including how interaction with values and practices with regard to literacy and to disability occurs.

As these suggestions are very much in line with my own feelings, they acted as a helpful additional stimulus to the research project described in this book.

My next aim, therefore, was to attempt to illuminate the ways in which the learning careers of children manifesting learning difficulties of a dyslexic nature contributed to the strong possibility that by the age of transfer to secondary school they were already identifying themselves as academic 'losers' who were at risk of carrying that self-inflicted label with them throughout the rest of their lives. My colleague Julia Burdett and I approached this task by constructing an interview schedule which focused on the key events relating to dyslexic children's growing awareness of their specific difficulties and their feelings of being (mis)understood by significant others such as parents, teachers and peers. At the same time we decided to gather further confirmatory data by employing a standardized technique for identifying learning self-concept (the Myself-as-a-Learner Scale), and by drawing upon recent learning and motivational theories to construct two complementary questionnaires relating to dyslexics' feelings of self-efficacy, learned helplessness and depression, together with their sense of being understood, their satisfactions and dissatisfactions and their attributions for success and failure. Further rich data were gathered by asking people with dyslexia to provide personal metaphors for dyslexia in the form of 'pictures in the mind'.

Once these theory-based techniques for investigating the sense of learning identity held by dyslexics had been selected and constructed, the next task was to try them out on a suitable population. A fortunate opportunity was provided to interview a significant number of dyslexic boys (50) between the ages of 11 and 16 attending a specialist residential school. The ways in which those interviews were carried out and their results analysed have been described in Chapters 4 and 5. Interestingly, the outcomes of this investigation did not turn out quite as expected because, basically, the school proved to be outstanding in what it set out to do, i.e. to turn dyslexic 'losers' into academic and sporting 'winners'. What our interviews showed, in contrast to most previous research studies, was that with the right kind of educational provision people with dyslexia do not necessarily have to suffer from lifelong feelings of learned helplessness or depression but can develop strong feelings of self-efficacy and internal locus of control which can make a powerful contribution towards academic success at 16. We draw upon another theory from social science, Ajzen's theory of planned behaviour, to help account for some of the reasons for this transformation. Noteworthy here also is Pollard's emphasis upon three key elements of learning stance – *motivation*, *self-confidence* and *strategic resources*. 'Together these accumulate to give a learner a sense of control, or otherwise in a learning situation' (Pollard, 1996, p. 88).

Whatever else they may do, the results of the study described in this book do provide considerable pause for thought about many of the difficulties associated with growing up dyslexic. What they enable us to do firstly is to question some of the assumptions about the nature of dyslexic identity that have arisen from the results of much of the previous research in this area. Contrary to common belief, we have found that although being faced with specific learning difficulties of a dyslexic nature is highly likely to have a negative effect on a person's academic self-concept, this does not necessarily lead to feelings of learned helplessness or depression of a long-standing nature. On the contrary, the majority of dyslexic adolescents in our study show signs of having survived within the education system somewhat battered but unbowed. They did not, on the whole, suffer from being bullied or shunned by other children because of their dyslexia, but did have to find ways of coping with a continuing amount of mainstream teachers' ignorance, usually with the help and support of much more 'clued up' mothers and the all-too-few specially trained teachers. Whether they would have continued to cope within mainstream secondary schools, even with strong specialist support, should be the topic of another study, especially since appropriate techniques are now available.

What we can state with some confidence, however, is that even those dyslexic students who unfortunately do have to struggle to survive emotionally intact through their early school years are not necessarily destined to a future of failure, low self-esteem and despair. There is no doubt that they can be helped to achieve success on a number of fronts provided that they are afforded not only good instruction in how to overcome their learning difficulties but also psychological input of a particular kind.

The average of group scores on meaningful tests and questionnaires can be extremely illuminating but it can also obscure the unique ways in which individuals perceive their worlds and the factors that contribute to this. A further section has therefore been included in which the personal histories of several of the boys interviewed have been presented. The main purpose of these accounts is to show the similarities and differences in the background experiences of fairly typical dyslexics and the ways in which they made sense of those experiences in constructing their personal interpretations of what it means to be dyslexic.

The question remains as to whether a negative self-concept precedes learning difficulties or vice versa. There is a growing weight of evidence to indicate that the relationship is by no means straightforward, but that academic self-concept begins to develop as a result of one's successes and failures during the early school years where it is mediated by the reactions of significant others. Over time this relationship becomes more reciprocal, with a developing positive or negative image of oneself as a learner gradually beginning to affect one's motivation to learn and one's feelings of self-efficacy and/or learned helplessness, which in turn contributes to one's effectiveness in learning situations.

Therefore, the natural sequence of events to reverse this tendency would be to build up feelings of self-efficacy whilst providing the necessary skills and strategies to overcome the specific learning difficulties, which in turn will begin to have an effect on the learning self-concept. This suggests that changes in one's sense of autonomy and agency are important precursors, or at least initially important early stages, in the reconstruction of one's identity as a successful learner. The final stage of this process is likely to be the establishment of a securely positive and realistic academic self-concept.

This inevitably leads to the further question as to how this can best be accomplished. As we have seen, Ajzen's theory of planned behaviour suggests that the three key aspects of positive intention, internal locus of control, and a shared environmental ethos can contribute a significant amount to any learning outcomes. With this in mind, it can be argued that an important set of presage factors for dyslexics turning the corner are (a) the intention and determination to overcome their difficulties, (b) the belief that their future success lies in their own hands, and (c) the kind of learning environment in which others with a similar set of goals work together to help each other to achieve success. As Pollard (1996) points out, there is a need for the provision of a social context in which there are opportunities to learn and in which children are enabled to exercise some control over their construction of meaning and understanding, together with high quality teaching and assistance in learning.

My intention throughout has been to highlight the psychosocial nature of dyslexia whilst focusing on aspects of dyslexics' sense of identity that are all too often overlooked. I firmly believe that a person with underlying dyslexic difficulties is more than just a poor reader, speller or mathematician. The experience of being faced with such difficulties, the way in which the symptoms are recognized and understood by significant others, and the social, psychological and educational consequences of formal diagnosis all play a part in contributing to the individual's sense of identity. One becomes, in effect, a different person.

It is clear from published personal accounts and from our own considerable experience in talking to and working with dyslexics of all ages that the condition continues to carry a stigma. In the terms of the sociologist Erving Goffman, many dyslexic people feel *marginalized*. Traditionally, this carries with it feelings of embarrassment and shame. Many dyslexics therefore seek to 'pass' by refusing to acknowledge their condition to others and by developing strategies to cover up the difficulties with which they are faced.

The result of our interviews with the students attending the specialist school for dyslexics, however, showed signs of a very different picture emerging – one of dyslexic *pride*. This was undoubtedly influenced by the unprecedented success rate achieved in public examinations over several years and the excellent sporting achievements of the various school teams and individual athletes. However, we were also able to infer from the boys' accounts and the interactions between teachers and students which we observed that this success was predicated by other factors.

A considerable body of research now exists into what makes an 'effective' school, dating back at least 25 years to the publication of *Fifteen Thousand Hours* by Michael Rutter and his colleagues (Rutter et al., 1979). Much of this research has been summarized by Teddlie and Reynolds in their massive *International Handbook of School Effectiveness Research* (2000), where they claim to have identified a number of key factors that contribute to school effectiveness. This approach is not without its critics, however. Wrigley (2004), for example, suggests that a number of writers have shown their concern about the reductionism implicit in much school effectiveness research. As he explains (p. 228) 'it seems indisputable that some schools achieve greater success, in examination and test results but also in terms of a wider view of educational achievement, than other schools in similar environments. The problem lies rather in an inadequate articulation of what counts as success, why some schools achieve it to a greater degree, and how other schools may aspire towards it.'

In keeping with the social interactionist perspective taken throughout this book, my interpretation of the success achieved by this particular school is based upon what I see as the natural application of *mediated learning experiences* (MLE) as described by Reuven Feuerstein and his colleagues (Feuerstein et al., 1991; Kozulin and Rand, 2000; Seng et al., 2003). Feuerstein has identified 12 principles which he considers to be essential prerequisites of an effective teaching–learning process. Considerable research now attests to the significant impact on the quality of learning outcomes for learners of all ages and (dis)abilities following the application of these principles (Burden, 2000a; Klein, 2000; Kozulin, 2000; Kang and Tan, 2003; Shamir, 2003).

A brief summary of the principles of MLE will now be provided together with a commentary on how these can be seen to relate to the development of a positive sense of identity in young people faced with learning difficulties of a dyslexic nature.

Principles of mediated learning experience

1.   The principle of *intentionality and reciprocity*, i.e. the need to make clear exactly what one's intentions are as a teacher with regard to learning outcomes, and to ensure that one's students are ready, willing and committed to participating in the same enterprise.

2.   The principle of mediating for *meaning*, i.e. to ensure that any learning activity is seen to have significance by the learners and is valued by them. Any activity that is not meaningful is likely to be, by definition, considered of little or no worth.

3.   The principle of *transcendence*, whereby learning activities are understood to have significance beyond the here and now in time and space.

If we relate these first three essential elements of mediated learning experience to the development of a strong sense of positive identity as a learner in children with dyslexic difficulties, we can readily see the importance of their teachers and parents establishing with them right from the start the value of literacy in its own right as well as its significance to their future life opportunities, whilst at the same time establishing a contract with them as to exactly how they will work together to achieve jointly agreed aims. Literacy is not something that can be imposed upon or even imparted to learners. It is rather a process of joint construction which goes far beyond the transmission of any reading or spelling programme, however well structured. Thus it is essential to foster as early as possible a shared enjoyment of books of all kinds as well as the significance of the written and print-ed word. The point here is that children must want to learn to read and write or type and will only be intrinsically and extrinsically moti-vated to do so if they can see some immediate and long-term purpose in it for them. Focusing heavily upon skills training without this underlying motivation will lead only to limited success at best.

There are nine other recognized aspects of MLE, all of which in their own way will provide added impetus to the learning process.

4.   The mediation of *feelings of competence* is the next principle, which can be seen to relate directly to a sense of self-efficacy in contrast to feelings of learned helplessness. This has been a major theme running throughout this book and should need no further explication here except to reinforce the point that this will not be achieved by simplistic and inappropriate rewards or uninformed praise. The best way to help achieve feelings of competence is to provide informative feedback, reinforcing appropriately used skills and strategies and pointing out where and why mistakes have occurred by their lack of or inappropriate use.

5.   The importance of viewing problems as *challenges* exemplifies
     the next principle, one that has been beautifully illustrated in the
     work of the motivational theorist Csikszentmihalyi in his descrip-
     tion of the 'flow' learning experience, when one becomes so
     absorbed in the learning process that time seems to stand still
     (Csikszentmihalyi and Csikszentmihalyi, 1988). The importance
     for the dyslexic here is the reconstruction of a problem into a
     challenge to the point at which they take on an active role in
     seeking learning challenges rather than shying away from what
     they have come to see as insurmountable problems. According to
     Csikszentmihalyi, a challenge occurs when one's interest in a
     topic or activity is matched by the requirement to extend one's
     skills just beyond the level at which one feels competent. Thus,
     there is little point in providing children with dyslexic difficulties
     with work that is uninteresting or too easy for them because this
     provides no challenge and they become bored. Equally, if the
     work is far beyond their present capabilities, they are likely to
     become frustrated and to give up.

6.   *Goal seeking, goal setting* and *goal achieving* have come to be
     recognized also by many motivation theorists (e.g. Ames, 1992)
     as vitally important to learning. As well as helping the learner to
     focus upon desired learning outcomes in a realistic manner, this
     aspect of mediation also contributes towards a strong sense of
     learning autonomy. The research evidence suggests that a signif-
     icant contributor to the growth of feelings of learned
     helplessness amongst people with dyslexia, and adolescents in
     particular, is the lack of (academic) goals. If by the age of 11 or
     12 a young person has already given up on the likelihood of
     achieving any form of examination success, then the future must
     appear very bleak, particularly in view of the current emphasis
     within UK schools on the importance of examination grades. In
     order to rectify such feelings, the dyslexic student needs first to
     be helped to see the importance of setting personal goals, not
     just in academic areas, then to set realistic short-term goals, pos-
     sibly at first with regard to completing a piece of work in a given
     time period, gradually increasing their targeted work whilst
     decreasing the amount of time to be taken. The special school we
     observed was particularly adept at encouraging its dyslexic stu-
     dents to select a sporting activity in which they were particularly

interested and to set personal goals for increasing their skills and achievements. In this way, as through the visual and performing arts, the mediation of goal seeking, setting and achieving can gradually be introduced into the academic sphere also.

7.   The mediation of the need to see one's behaviour as within one's *control* once again links in with previously described research and theory on people's attributions for success and failure, particularly those aspects that reveal the benefits of having a strong sense of internal locus of control. Those who see themselves as capable of taking control over what happens in their lives are far more likely to be high achievers at school and in the workplace and less likely to manifest disturbed or troublesome behaviour. This can only be achieved by providing opportunities for young people to take on a sense of responsibility for their own actions and be trusted to act in an appropriate manner. Students with dyslexia will inevitably display a strong need at first for considerable help and support with their work, but unless they are gradually weaned away from this dependency they are likely to falter when required to stand on their own two feet.

8.   The importance of fostering *awareness of change* as an essential aspect of the human condition encourages learners to reflect upon how and why their lives have changed in various ways, are contributing to change, and, most importantly, are capable of changing in directions that they themselves envisage. This aspect of mediation emphasizes the fact that nobody needs to remain 'stuck' in a situation not of their own making. It is therefore important for students with dyslexia to learn how to monitor for themselves the progress they are making as they develop greater phonic awareness, learn to analyse and synthesize sounds and phonemes, and improve their spelling and/or mathematics strategies. The use of personal charts recording small steps successfully accomplished as well as significant goals achieved can be extremely helpful in this respect, as also are portfolios of creative and other work.

9/10. Two further complementary aspects of MLE are the encouragement of recognition of the individual as a unique person in their own right (*individuation*) and the importance of *sharing* with others. Dyslexics need to be helped to feel that they are in some way special, with unique talents that transcend the difficulties they are encountering with literacy or numeracy such that their overall sense of personal identity overrides any specific negative feelings about their literacy difficulties. At the same time, they need to be helped to see that by sharing their problems with others, as well as sharing the strategies that they have found helpful in overcoming or circumventing specifically difficult learning tasks, they can empower both themselves and others. This is where the notion of dyslexic pride becomes particularly pertinent. Rather than feeling embarrassment or shame, people with dyslexia need to be helped to recognize their own unique talents and to see that they have a great deal to offer to others who may well be less fortunate than they are in a variety of different ways. Paradoxical as it may seem, some of the best mentors of children with dyslexia are others who have learnt how to deal with the same problems.

11. This relates directly to the mediation of a sense of *belonging*, the importance of feeling that we are part of a group of people, family or friends, who understand how we feel about issues that matter to us and can both give and receive appropriate support when needed. This is one of the central elements of Ajzen's theory of planned behaviour and an aspect of the specialist school for dyslexics that stood out in our study. We have seen this illustrated earlier in the quotes about the school provided by some of the students. It was also shown in the success of the school's sports teams and in the celebration of their successes in the termly newsletters to parents and friends of the school.

     If inclusion is to become reality in mainstream schools rather than merely a philosophical slogan, then such schools will need to foster feelings of belonging in all their students, especially these with special educational needs (Avramidis et al., 2002; Griffiths et al., 2004).

12. The final currently recognized aspect of MLE is the need to foster the belief in *optimistic alternatives*. As has been indicated earlier in this book, a significant current trend amongst psychologists is to move away from an emphasis upon such explanatory states as learned helplessness and pessimism towards identifying factors contributing to resilience and the positive benefits of optimism (Seligman, 1991; Luthar et al., 2000). Recent therapeutic

techniques such as cognitive therapy (Beck, 1993) and solution-focused brief therapy (Stobie et al., 2005) extol the benefits of taking such an approach and provide considerable evidence of its effectiveness. It may well be that some of those struggling to overcome their dyslexic difficulties would benefit from counselling or even therapy of this nature, as was indicated in the sample of dyslexic students whom we interviewed. What is undoubtedly true, however, is that an optimistic outlook on life and view of the future is particularly important for dealing with the stresses of everyday life and for achieving successful outcomes in any form of endeavour. Basically, anyone suffering from difficulties of a dyslexic nature has to be helped to construct an underlying belief system that things can and will ultimately get better. It is on this foundation that the other aspects of mediated learning experiences can be built.

These aspects of mediated learning theory have been described here for a number of reasons. They provide what we consider to be essential complementary aspects of any intervention with dyslexic children and adults to the more traditional content-based approach, or even one that emphasizes the process of multi-sensory teaching. They also help us to see how and why successful educational provision for dyslexics can be accomplished, as exemplified by our specialist school. What we have here is an educational philosophy that has been shown to work in practice, especially in the establishment of a powerful sense of learner identity.

To return to the point from which we began, it is my belief that the vitally important socio-cultural aspect of dyslexia has hitherto been unjustifiably neglected in research studies in this area. This can be seen, in particular, in the ways in which children struggling to overcome specific learning difficulties in becoming literate develop a sense of 'dyslexic identity' as a result of their educational experiences and interactions with significant others. At the same time, comparatively few opportunities have been afforded dyslexic young people to give voice to their thoughts and feelings about growing up dyslexic, although this situation shows signs of beginning to change (Humphrey, 2002; Johnson and Peer, 2004).

What literature does exist suggests that one possible reason for this neglect may well have been the absence of useful assessment techniques. This book has demonstrated that such techniques do exist and can be constructed on the foundation of modern psychological learning theory, and that they can provide invaluable information not only about the current psychological well-being of any dyslexic individual but also as a means of evaluating the quality of the educational provision being offered to dyslexic students. There would appear to be no reason, therefore, why future research and interventions in the broad domain of dyslexia should not continue to expand by drawing upon psychosocial theory to the benefit of all.

References

Abramson LY, Seligman MEP, Teasdale JD (1978) Learned helplessness in humans: Critique and reformulation. Journal of Abnormal Psychology 87: 49–74.

Ajzen I (1991) Attitudes, personality and behaviour. Milton Keynes: Open University Press.

Ames C (1992) Classrooms; goals, structures and student motivation. Journal of Educational Psychology 84(3): 261–271.

Armitage CJ, Conner M (2001) Efficacy of the theory of planned behaviour: A meta-analytic review. British Journal of Social Psychology 40: 471–499.

Avramidis E, Bayliss P, Burden R L (2002) Inclusion in action: an in-depth case study of an inclusive secondary school in the South-west of England. International Journal of Inclusive Education 6(2): 143–163.

Bandura A (1986) Social Foundations of Thought and Action: A Social Cognitive Theory. Englewood Cliffs, NJ: Prentice Hall.

Bandura A (1997) Self-efficacy: The exercise of control. New York: WH Freeman.

Bandura A, Pastorelli C, Barbaranelli C, Caprara GV (1999) Self-efficacy pathways to childhood depression. Journal of Personality and Social Psychology 76: 258–269.

Bar-Tal D, Darom E (1979) Pupils' attributions of success and failure. Child Development 50: 264–267.

Beck AT (1993) Cognitive therapy: Past, present and future. Journal of Consulting and Clinical Psychology 61: 194–198.

Black M (1979) More about metaphor. In: Ortony A (ed.) Metaphor and Thought. Cambridge: Cambridge University Press.

Borkowski JG, Weyhing RS, Carr M (1988) Effects of attribution retraining on strategy-based reading comprehension in learning-disabled students. Journal of Educational Psychology 80: 46–53.

Bruner J (1996) The Culture of Education. Cambridge, MA: Harvard University Press.

Burden RL (1998) Assessing children's perceptions of themselves as learners and problem-solvers: The construction of the Myself-As-a-Learner Scale. School Psychology International 19(4): 291–305.

Burden RL (2000a) Feuerstein's unique contribution to educational and school psychology. In: Kozulin A, Rand Y (eds) Experiences of Medicated Learning. Oxford: Pergamon.

Burden RL (2000b) The Myself-as-a-Learner Scale (MALS). Windsor: NFER-Nelson.

Burns RB (1982) Self-concept Development and Education. London: Holt, Rinehart and Winston.

Butkowsky TS, Willows DM (1980) Cognitive motivation and characteristics of children varying in reading ability; evidence of learned helplessness in poor readers. Journal of Educational Psychology 72: 408–422.

Bynner J, Ekynsmith C (1994) Young Adults' Literacy and Numeracy Problems: Some evidence from the British Cohort Study. London: ALBSU.

Byrne BM (1996) Measuring Self-Concept Across the Life-span. Washington: American Psychological Association.

Carr M, Borkowski JG, Maxwell SE (1991) Motivational components of underachievement. Developmental Psychology 27: 108–118.

Chapman JW (1988a) Learning disabled children's self-concepts. Review of Educational Research 58: 347–371.

Chapman JW (1988b) Cognitive-motivational characteristics and academic achievement of learning disabled children: A longitudinal study. Journal of Educational Psychology 80: 357–365.

Coles GS (1987) The Learning Mystique: A Critical Look at Learning Disabilities. New York: Pantern Books.

Cooley CH (1912) Human Nature and the Social Order. New York: Scribners.

Craske ML (1988) Learned helplessness, self-worth motivation and attribution retraining for primary school children. British Journal of Educational Psychology 20(4): 15–36.

Csikszentmihalyi M, Csikszentmihalyi IS (eds) (1988) Optimal Experience. Cambridge: Cambridge University Press.

de Charms R (1976) Enhancing Motivation: Change in the Classroom. New York: Halstead.

Edwards J (1994) The Scars of Dyslexia. London: Cassell.

Erikson E (1959) Identity and the Life Cycle. New York: IVP.

Fairhurst P, Pumfrey PD (1992) Secondary school organisation and the self-concepts of pupils with relative reading difficulties. Research in Education 47: 17–27.

Feuerstein R, Klein PS, Tannenbaum AJ (1991) Mediated Learning Experience: Theoretical, Psychological, and Learning Implications. London: Freund.

Findley MJ, Cooper HM (1983) Locus of control and academic achievement: a literature review. Journal of Personal and Social Psychology 42(2): 419–427.

Fishbein M, Ajzen I (1975) Belief, Attitude, Intention and Behaviour: An Introduction to Theory and Research. Reading, MA: Addison-Wesley.

Frederickson N, Jacobs S (2001) Controllability attributions for academic performance and the perceived scholastic competence, global self-worth and achievement of children with dyslexia. School Psychology International 22(4): 401–416.

Gerber PJ, Schneiders CA, Paradise LV et al. (1990) Persisting problems of adults with learning disabilities: self-reported comparisons from their school age and adult years. Journal of Learning Disabilities 23: 570–573.

Gilbert P (1992) Depression: The Evolution of Powerlessness. Hillsdale, NJ: Erlbaum.

Gjessing HJ, Karlsen B (1989) A Longitudinal Study of Dyslexia. New York: Springer.

Goffman E (1968) Stigma: Notes on the Management of Spoiled Identity. Harmondsworth: Penguin.

Griffiths C, Norwich B, Burden RL (2004) 'I'm glad that I don't take no for an answer': Parent–professional relationships and dyslexia. Research Report on behalf of the Buttle Trust and the British Dyslexia Association: Exeter University School of Education.

Hansford BL, Hattie JA (1982) The relationship between self and achievement/performance measures. Review of Educational Research 52: 123–142.

Herrington M, Hunter-Carsch M (2001) A social interactive model of specific learning difficulties, e.g. dyslexia. In: Hunter-Carsch M (ed.) Dyslexia: A Psychosocial perspective. London: Whurr.

Huberman AM, Miles MB (1994) Data management and analysis methods. In: Denzin NK, Lincoln YS (eds) Handbook of Qualitative Research. London: Sage.

Humphrey N (2002) Teacher and pupil ratings of self-esteem in developmental dyslexia. British Journal of Special Education 29(1): 29–36.

Humphrey N, Mullins PM (2002) Personal constructs and attribution for academic success and failure in dyslexia. British Journal of Special Education 29(4): 196–203.

Jacobson B, Lowery P, Du Cette J (1986) Attributions of learning disabled children. Journal of Educational Psychology 78: 59–64.

Johnson M, Peer L (2004) Pupils' concept of dyslexia friendly teaching. Paper delivered to International Dyslexia Conference, Warwick, July.

Joiner TE, Wagner KD (1995) Attribution style and depression in children and adolescents: a meta-analytic review. Clinical Psychology Review 15(8): 777–798.

Kang Y, Tan O (2003) Improving the cognitive performance of children with disabilities: A case of mediation. In: Seng A, Pou L, Tan O (eds) Mediated Learning Experience with Children. Singapore: McGraw Hill.

Kistner JA, Osbourne M, Le Verrier L (1988) Causal attributions of learning disabled progress. Journal of Educational Psychology 80: 82–89.

Klein PS (2000) A mediational approach to early intervention. In: Kozulin A, Rand Y (eds) Experience of Mediated Learning. Oxford: Pergamon

Kozulin A (2000) The diversity of Instrumental Enrichment applications. In: Kozulin A, Rand Y (eds) Experience of Mediated Learning. Oxford: Pergamon.

Kozulin A, Rand Y (eds) (2000) Experience of Mediated Learning. Oxford: Pergamon.

Leary ED (ed.) (1999) Metaphors in the History of Psychology. Cambridge: Cambridge University Press.

Lerner JW (2000) Learning Disabilities: Theories, Diagnosis and Teaching Strategies, 8th edn. Boston: Houghton Mifflin.

Lewandowski L, Arcangelo K (1994) The social adjustment and self-concept of adults with learning disabilities. Journal of Learning Disabilities 27: 598–605.

Luthar SS, Cicchetti D, Becker B (2000). The construct of resilience: A critical evaluation and guidelines for future work. Child Development 71(3): 543–562.

Maughan B (1994). Behaviour development and reading disability. In: Hulme C, Snowling M (eds) Reading Development and Dyslexia. London: Whurr.

Murray L, Woolgar M, Cooper P (2001) Cognitive vulnerability to depression in 5-year-old children of depressed mothers. Journal of Child Psychology and Psychiatry 42(7): 891–900.

Osmond J (1993) The Reality of Dyslexia. London: Cassell.

Ozik C (1986) The moral necessity of metaphor: Rooting history in a figure of speech. Harper's 272: 62–68.

Pajares F (1999) Current directions in self-efficacy research. www.emory.edu/EDUCATION/mpf/effchapter.htm.

Pollard A (with Filer A) (1996) The School World of Children's Learning. London: Cassell.

Reed ES (2001) Towards a cultural ecology of instruction. In: Bakhurst D, Skanker SG (eds) Jerome Bruner: Language, Culture, Self. London: Sage, pp. 116–126.

Resnick MJ, Harter S (1989) Impact of social comparisons on the developing self-perceptions of learning disabled students. Journal of Educational Psychology 81: 631–638.

Riddick B, Sterling C, Farmer M, Morgan S (1999) Self-esteem and anxiety in the educational histories of adult dyslexic students. Dyslexia 5: 227–248.

Rogers CR (1951) Client-Centred Therapy. Boston: Houghton Mifflin.

Rotter JB (1954) Social Learning and Clinical Psychology. Englewood Cliffs, NJ: Prentice Hall.

Rutter M, Maughan B, Mortimore P, Ouston J (1979) Fifteen Thousand Hours: Secondary Schools and their Effects on Children. London: Open Books.

Saracoglu B, Minden H, Wilchesky M (1989) The adjustment of students with learning disabilities to university and its relationship to self-esteem and self-efficacy. Journal of Learning Disabilities 22: 590–592.

Schunk DH (1983) Developing children's self-efficacy and skills: The roles of social comparative information and goal setting. Contemporary Educational Psychology 8: 76–86.

Schunk DH (1984) Self-efficacy perspective on achievement behaviour. Educational Psychologist 19: 48–58.

Schunk DH (1991) Self-efficacy and academic motivation. Educational Psychologist 26: 207–231.

Seligman MEP (1975) Helplessness: On Depression Development and Death. San Francisco: Freeman.

Seligman MEP (1991) Learned Optimism. New York: Knopf.

Seligman MEP, Abramson LY, Semmel A, Baeyer CV (1979) Depressive attributional style. Journal of Abnormal Psychology 88: 242–247.

Seng AS, Pou LK, Tan O (2003) Mediated Learning Experience with Children: Applications across contexts. Singapore: McGraw Hill.

Sfard A (1998) On two metaphors for learning and the dangers of choosing just one. Educational Researcher 27(2): 4–13.

Shamir A (2003) Peer mediation with young children: An intervention program. In: Seng A, Pou L, Tan O (eds) Mediated Learning Experience with Children. Singapore: McGraw Hill.

Skaalvik EM, Hagvet KA (1990) Academic achievement and self-concept: An analysis of causal predominance in a developmental perspective. Journal of Personality and Social Psychology 58: 292–307.

Stanovich KE (1986). Matthew effects in reading: Some consequences of individual differences in the acquisition of literacy. Reading Research Quarterly 21: 73–113.

Stobie I, Boyle J, Woolfson L (2005) Solution-focused approaches in the practice of UK educational psychologists: A study of the nature of their applications and evidence of their effectiveness. School Psychology International 26(1): 5–28.

Sutton S (1998) Predicting and explaining intentions and behaviour. Journal of Applied Social Psychology 28: 1317–1338.

Teddlie C, Reynolds D (2000) International Handbook of School Effectiveness Research. London: Routledge Falmer.

Thomson M (1990) Developmental Dyslexia. London: Whurr.

Thomson M, Hartley GM (1980) Self-esteem in dyslexic children. Academic Therapy 16: 19–36.

Van Overwalle F, de Metsenaere M (1990) The effects of attribution-based intervention and study strategy training on academic achievement in college freshmen. British Journal of Educational Psychology 60: 299–311.

Wertsch J (1992) Culture, Communication and Cognition. Cambridge: Cambridge University Press.

Williams MD, Burden RL, Lanvers U (2002) 'French is the language of love and stuff': Student perceptions of issues related to motivation in learning a foreign language. British Educational Research Journal 28(4): 503–528.

Wrigley T (2004) 'School effectiveness'; the problem of reductionism. British Educational Research Journal 30(2): 227–244.

Zimmerman BJ (1995) Self-efficacy and educational development. In: Bandura A (ed.) Self-efficacy in Changing Societies. New York: Cambridge University Press, pp. 202–231.

Zimmerman IL, Allegrand GN (1965) Personality characteristics and attitudes forward achievement of good and poor readers. Journal of Educational Research 59: 28–30.

Index

Printed in the United Kingdom by
Lightning Source UK Ltd., Milton Keynes
138372UK00001B/140/P